GETTING PUBLISHED

How to Learn and Master
the Business of Writing

GETTING PUBLISHED

How to Learn and Master the Business of Writing

By DAVID MAGEE

jefferson press

ISBN 0–97189–743–3
Library of Congress Catalog Card Number: 2006921090

Edited by Henry Oehmig
Book Design by Fiona Raven

First Printing May 2006
Printed in U.S.A.

Published by Jefferson Press

jefferson press

P.O. Box 115
Lookout Mountain, TN 37350

For my wife,
who always believed I would succeed as an author.

Contents

Introduction

No matter what subject I use as the basis of talks to various groups around the country — whether discussing books I have written about John Deere, professional golfer Phil Mickelson, international business executive Carlos Ghosn, or Ford Motor Company — the same common themes emerge in question and answer sessions that follow.

People are satisfied enough to learn more about subjects of history or current events, but most of all, what they really want to know is what advice I can give them that will ease their quest to become a bona fide published author. Without fail, when a talk is over and listeners line up to buy a signed book or shake a hand, two or three out of four are quick to tell me that they, too, are either hoping to write a book soon or have written one and want to know if I will help them find an agent, publisher, or both.

Before becoming an author myself, I had heard generalizations that "everybody wants to write a book" but dismissed this as a ridiculous exaggeration. Now that I have become one, however, and have been exposed on a somewhat regular basis to an inquiring public, I am at least convinced that this is three-quarters true. Everybody may not want to write and have a book published, but it certainly appears that the vast majority do. And after fielding inquiries from many for tips in how to make it happen, I have concluded that most people have no idea of what to do or where to turn.

They feel shut out by an industry that cloisters itself behind a seemingly impenetrable wall of rejection. Many would-be writers are so desperate to find an "in" to the industry that they will ask for anything from tips to general information to agent or editor recommendations from the author held captive at a signing table. A generally compassionate sort who enjoys helping people, my style has been to listen best as I can while providing helpful tidbits in small doses. If the persistent have not been able to get enough useful help in such small doses, I typically resort to dishing out my e-mail address, suggesting they contact me later.

The problem with both of these responses, however, is that the business of book writing is one of the most difficult to crack. In giving short responses, I have really offered little of use because bits and pieces are not much help at all for those who know little to none about how to get published by a mainstream house. And the time it takes to give full responses is something I really do not have the luxury of. Far too often, I have given out an e-mail address, only to get requests for information that are so extensive I cannot adequately respond.

My career as a full-time writer, president and part-owner of a publishing company, and father to three active children leaves little in the way of free time to develop careers outside of my own. Besides, I am a publishing professional, and this business is how I make my money. I get paid as a writer, as a consultant, and as a publisher. That is how I feed my family. If a lawyer wants to write a book, but cannot figure out how, he should not expect me to deliver a free road map any more than I should expect him to provide me pro-bono legal work.

My resolution to this challenge came as an epiphany after one particularly grueling signing. The answer was not to turn away those seeking help or to charge them exorbitant consulting fees.

———————————————— oOo ————————————————

Instead, I was struck by the writer's natural inclination. If those trying to become a published author themselves think I have something valuable to offer in the way of professional advice, the best option would be to use my craft and explain in a book my experiences and thoughts on the business of writing. The result is that readers can get information that hopefully is useful and beneficial to their cause and I can receive the compensation that any author considers fair — royalties.

You want to know how to get an agent? Want to know how I got my first publishing contract? Want to know what a proposal should look like? Want to know how to best communicate with an editor?

Simply buy the book.

My challenge, of course, is providing substantive information that has not been presented before. There are so many magazines, web sites, conferences and books in print available to the would-be writer that it can become a blur of repetitive overload. Advice is available in the form of everything from how best to communicate with agents to what consists of good non-fiction writing to what style creates good fiction characters. This is all good, and valuable, if the writer can differentiate the meaningful from the meaningless, but I have learned that it still leaves most in a kind of purgatory place. They have a little bit more understanding of the trade, but they have no idea if they are closer to getting published or have no chance whatsoever — and they do not know what to do about it.

This is where I come in. *Getting Published* is an approach that deals with book writing from the proper perspective that it is a business. To cross over the transom and into this realm, a

———————————————— oOo ————————————————

———————— oOo ————————

writer, in most instances, needs a full understanding of all that is involved and why. The ability to put mere words on paper is usually not enough. There are simply so many people trying to write books in this world that you cannot talk or walk your way into a contract from HarperCollins, Random House or Simon and Schuster, nor will your best poetry get the job done.

In most instances, skill and a full understanding and respect of the way publishing works as a business are required to make the transition from a would-be writer to a full-fledged, published author with a contract from a reputable house with books on shelves of the largest retailers and the most prominent libraries in the country. If you possess it all — an ability to write and a workable knowledge of the business — the odds of succeeding are still stacked against you. If a writer has one, without the other, the odds are slimmer yet. But if you have neither skill nor an understanding of the business, the challenge will prove next to impossible.

I cannot make any readers of this work a great writer when I am not even a great writer myself. My hope, though, is to offer some broad guidelines, allowing you to be able to frame your talent and work in a more appropriate light. For instance, if one's word-skill is mid-level and their dream is to become a bestselling fiction author, one might decide after reading *Getting Published* that their calling is in fact to be a non-fiction writer, where prose is typically not judged with such a discerning eye. Or, a highly skilled writer hoping to sell a million self-help books may decide after reading this book that they are too shy and unmarketable to realize that dream, turning to more creative, literary means to tell their story instead.

———————— oOo ————————

Often, these are the differences in getting published or not for hopeful writers. And far too frequently, a person decides they want to be an author and pushes forward with a narrow mindset of what type of book will be successful, without taking the time to analyze with any objectivity or educated wisdom whether or not it makes sense from a business perspective.

And that is why this work is now available, an attempt at offering an honest guide from a writer's perspective to what many people consider the most difficult industry to break into. Foremost, it is intended to provide understanding of the industry and the struggle to get published in a manner that has not been readily available before.

When I made the decision to become a full-time writer some years ago, I went in search of helpful information in book form and found dozens upon dozens of choices. The problem was that successful writers typically approaching the subject of writing left out many of the more informative details needed by hopefuls. Stephen King's *On Writing*, for example, is one of the best books on the craft that I have ever read. On several occasions I have moved from cover to cover in one sitting, seeking to adsorb knowledge from his insight and experience.

Many other more nuts-and-bolts advice books on writing and getting published are available, and I have found most of these have been written by less-than-successful writers. Some, in fact, appear to have obtained their first authorship byline the moment their how-to advice book rolled off the printing press. This is not to say these writers have little to offer, but would-be writers hoping to land their first contract might expect to learn more lessons from someone who has landed six-figure contracts and fully executed books from the aspects of writing, development of the sales and marketing plan, and in-the-field title promotion following publication.

I have scanned many of these available how-to books, holding onto valuable crumbs. The information retained was not nearly enough, however, and I grew weary of the patchwork guide I kept trying to piece together in my head from the various sources. Fortunately, at the time I sought a career as an author, I lived in a small Southern town which is rich in literary heritage and my local friends included writers, booksellers and even an agent who were successful in the industry, despite the fact that they resided far from New York geographically and even farther South colloquially.

Oxford, Mississippi had just more than 10,000 residents in the 1990s, but my friend and across-the-street-neighbor operated one of the top independent bookstores in all of America and served a term as president of the powerful American Booksellers Association. Growing up, my best friend down the street was a Faulkner, and his mother and father were both writers, though I had a hard time grasping what that really meant. Living in Oxford as an adult, I got to watch a friend named John Grisham begin a meteoric rise from small-time lawyer and state legislator to big-time, international bestselling author, just as I got to watch a local fireman and friend named Larry Brown emerge as one of the greatest Southern writers of our time. Not to mention another dozen or more writers who lived in the small town that had been published by or were in the process of writing books for large New York publishing houses.

Whenever I needed advice in the early stages of building

oOo

a foundation to launch a writing career, I could readily find it. When I needed inspiration as a reminder that my objective was attainable, I could readily find it. When I needed to drop a name to an agent or editor, I had them readily available at my disposal. My geographic presence hardly made my trip over the transom easy. Instead, this literary location provided layers of information in which I was able to seek, explore and learn, increasing my chances of getting published.

The information, along with a lot of luck, a little talent, a strong understanding of the importance and methods of good book marketing, and some excellent subjects, allowed me to earn advances and royalties totaling more than $400,000 during the first two-and-a-half years I was in the business. I had one book sell more than 100,000 copies worldwide and others published in multiple languages. More importantly, I was able to take my initial success and additional experience and morph into a new and more desired direction in terms of subject. And while I still have ideas that are turned down by publishers and the business will always be somewhat of a struggle because of its inherent difficulties, I am at least fortunate that I have what amounts to a couple of years of work lined up to keep me more than busy. Perhaps more importantly, I am also reaching the point in my career that I can write about subjects that are most appealing.

Of course, before a writer can reach the point of having backlogged work about exciting subjects, they have to make the critical transformation: from dreaming of a career to actually have a contract in hand from a legitimate publishing house. For most people, the only way this will occur, outside of blind luck, is when the would-be writer obtains a strong grasp on the

oOo

———————————— oOo ————————————

process, the expectations and the realities of the business. It is my most sincere hope that this small book helps many in this endeavor in a very big way.

———————————— oOo ————————————

If you want to be a writer
you must do two things above all others:
read a lot and write a lot.

— Stephen King

Chapter 1

Publishing is a Business

Writing may very well be an art, but unless you are producing manuscripts for the simple sake of contributing to the greater good and understanding of mankind, you must come face-to-face with the reality that it is unlikely anybody will ever want to publish your work unless they think they can make money by selling it. Publishing, after all, is a business. And profit is usually the single, driving force of enterprise.

At HarperCollins, Random House, Simon and Schuster and other publishing houses located in America and around the world, editors, managers and executives who cannot successfully oversee a line that contributes financial gain on both quarterly and an annual basis will quickly find themselves out

——————————— oOo ———————————

of work. It does not matter how important books may have been viewed as by readers or within the industry. With rare exception, if the works cannot or do not make money, they are labeled as unsuccessful.

This is a fact that most writers overlook when they begin to write their first manuscript or attempt to put their dream of becoming published into action. They view the actual writing as the single most important aspect of the professional and creative challenge. It is true, of course, that the publishing industry is based on the written word, and that if a person does not have talent, regardless of whether they are crafting fiction or non-fiction, crossing over the transom proves difficult. Though the reality is that if a want-to-be writer does not take the time to consider the business aspects of what they have to offer, how they should approach the industry, and what agents and editors are looking for, their chances of success — in what can be deemed a nearly impossible industry to crack even when all of the pieces are in place — drop precipitously.

When starting my journey toward the transom and attempting to cross it, I was fortunate to have been a business owner, an experience which helped me to gain a unique perspective of the demands of publishing. When there is payroll, office overhead and marketing and production costs to consider, there is a small chance that a company of any size will want to take a risk when the path to profit is not clear. Certainly, most editors and even many executives that work in the business have the highest appreciation for literary work of merit, but they are not exactly in a position these days to operate as charitable clearing houses for creativity. Recognizing this, when I definitively decided to

——————————— oOo ———————————

———————————————————— oOo ————————————————————

become a writer, I did not sit down at my computer and start rapping the keys with my first manuscript. Before hitting a keystroke, I took some time to look into and learn about the business aspects of publishing.

One of the first things a writer learns about the industry is that it has a very, very strong culture in place and that most editors and agents are creatures of habit who operate under a values-system that has been firmly adhered to for decades, and these experience very little change. Complain all you want about its rigors and try with all your might to get it to change and you will more likely than not find yourself still on the outside looking in. That does not mean, of course, that you operate somewhat out of the norm. Not only can you try different tricks, but they often work well as long as they fit within the framework of good business. Still, businesses like publishing with strong cultures are often impenetrable to the flagrantly disrespectful, and if you do not take the time to learn, understand and respect, it proves a difficult, if not impossible, business to enter.

Explore Bookstores

My approach was to start in bookstores, at the most basic level, shelf-shopping not for what I wanted to read, but to see what titles were being stocked, how they were displayed and how browsers were reacting to them. Authors so sure that they have the next great book in their head or on their computer may be shocked to learn how few books actually get displayed and how few new books are even actually stocked by book stores large and small. It just seems as if there are a myriad new titles and authors after one goes into a superstore, such as Barnes and

———————————————————— oOo ————————————————————

Noble, where hundreds to thousands of titles are available for purchase.

But to serve the masses, the stores cannot afford to stock every new author that comes out, and, therefore, many new books that have received acclaim and are published by the largest houses in the world are not even available. Shelves throughout the store have already been filled with titles in specific categories that were previously shipped, and the turn is not rapid. The new release tables for fiction and non-fiction typically are the best places to find new work, and not more than a few dozen can be squeezed into this valuable, limited space. If a book remains there for a few weeks with only tepid reader response, it is swiftly moved into the category aisles with other stocked titles.

When you walk in stores and browse aisles as a purveyor, not a buyer, it is easy to see how this works. Thousands and thousands of new titles are published each year, and not more than a few hundred find their way onto bookstore shelves in any mass quantity. The challenge is to determine which titles are moving and why and then make your first assessment of the business of writing. Immediately, you will understand what makes literary agents so reluctant to take on new projects: the little room for newcomers on bookstore shelves and most of them just occupying space, not selling. It is the old business rule of thumb that 10 percent of the product is delivering 90 percent of the sales and profit.

Agents, of course, rely on the acquisition of new titles because commission-based selling is their lifeblood. They may frequently act like they do not want new work, yet they have to take it. However, they can be extremely discerning considering it only makes sense to acquire what they strongly believe will sell to an editor or publishing house. And with so few books actually being stocked in stores in mass quantity, editors at even the largest houses are having a hard time acquiring and publishing profitably because that means many of their books are not getting needed exposure. Some people wrongly believe that just because Random House releases a title, Barnes and Noble will automatically stock thousands of copies as a no-brainer, but this is far from the truth.

Even the largest and most respected publishing houses have to fight season after season to show and prove that their titles deserve recognition and shelf space. With shelf space so tight, these publishers do not want to lessen their chances of having truly strong books garner less exposure due to over-crowding of available selling space from questionable titles. Consequently, they are apt to acquire very few new titles, seeking the homerun over the single or double. With larger publishers acquiring only so many new books each year, there are only so many manuscripts that the couple of hundred top agents in the industry can acquire from would-be authors as well. This is simply a matter of supply and demand that begins at the most basic level of books — the retail store.

The first thing a hopeful usually notices when looking hard at the shelf space in brick and mortar stores is that most of the new, stocked books belong to proven authors with a track record. This is due to the fact that when an announcement of a book is made by a publisher to bookstore buyers, the first thing the buyer typically does is base acquisition interests on previous

oOo

retail store sales. For example, if John Grisham sold 255,000 units of his last book through Barnes and Noble, buyers can make a safe assumption that his new book will sell close to the same. Plus, they can track areas throughout the country where sales were higher, or lower, and stock accordingly. As a new author with no track record, you can rightly assume from your bookstore visit that getting published can be a highly difficult proposition. John Grisham and Stephen King, as well as smaller names like David Magee and John T. Edge, have retail store sales records that publishers can rely on to forecast sales of one of their new titles.

Of course, brick and mortar bookstores are not the only places books are sold these days. It will help as well to heavily browse www.amazon.com and www.barnesandnoble.com to determine which titles are among the bestsellers. These places are also the best to get an idea of all the new books that are out since most fresh titles are listed online when many, even from large publishers, are non-existent in bookstores. It is also much easier and quicker to scan all titles on the Internet and do specific searches by author or genre or publisher. For example, I will often want to see what Simon and Schuster has in store for an upcoming season, and all I have to do is visit www.amazon .com, go to search, and enter the publisher's name, asking that all titles be listed by publication date. This shows everything the house has slated for the upcoming season as well as every new release from the current season. Change the search to Simon and Schuster's bestselling titles, and it is easy to assess which of the house's backlist books continue to move and which ones do not. Want to quickly find the bestselling automotive manuals, or the

oOo

bestselling Halloween titles or the bestselling cake-decorating books? It's all there on Amazon.com.

Do not be misled by the apparent success of some online books, however. A significant myth among many unpublished authors is that careers can be built from online sales. While there are case studies which bear this out, particularly in non-fiction books, in most instances, this assumption is false. Online book sales account for a significant portion of all titles sold each year, but, alone, they are not enough — unless, that is, you have a title sit at one of the top few spots at www.amazon.com for weeks on end. As a general rule, books ranking in the 2,000 to 20,000 range week-in, week-out will sell at Amazon.com not more than a couple of hundred units per month. So, if a writer has little or no quantifiable exposure in bookstores, there is little chance he or she can make ends meet on royalties from books sold in the traditional retail manner because their title will not have enough exposure.

Find Other Industry Research Sources
Beyond finding what books are being published and appear to be selling or not selling at the retail level, a study of the business of publishing must include trade materials and websites. Certainly this information is geared more toward the insider than the hopeful, yet it is imperative that writers understand what titles agents are acquiring, just as they should know which publishing houses are posting decent financial quarters and which ones are not.

In recent years, the emergence of www.publishersmarket place.com has proven to be a blessing for industry watchers

—————————————— oOo ——————————————

because it acts as a one-stop shopping place of information. No longer do we have to look in every corner around the world to piece together tidbits of useful information — they do it for us for a nominal monthly fee. Included in this site is reliable "deal" information, reporting new acquisitions by editors and publishers. This deal information typically lists the selling agent and the acquiring editor, as well as giving a hint as to the amount of the author advance provided under the contract terms.

The site also has frequently posted news updates, which can include wire stories of industry gossip, publisher financial reporting and personnel moves. There are also areas for Amazon .com sales trend watching and rights offerings posts. The publishing company that I founded and still hold active ownership in, Jefferson Press, has actually identified a potential project from this website, contacted the offering agent, and struck up a mutually satisfying deal. For hopeful authors, routine study of information posted on the site will ultimately provide an understanding of the business closer to what a veteran holds than a novice.

This does not mean you should strive to become so versed that you could hold a coffee or cocktail conversation with a New York editor. Instead, you want to gain enough knowledge so that when the time comes to pitch an agent, you might have enough background to suggest, "I think this book will fit nicely into John Doe's hands since he has been acquiring such titles."

There are other sources of information that will help you reach this point, such as *Publishers Weekly*, a trade magazine which is highly valuable but perhaps too in-depth for entry-level research. What the researcher wants to accomplish is a

—————————————— oOo ——————————————

—— oOo ——

general feel for trends, successes and failures in the industry. This information is more readily found in summary form on www.publishersmarketplace.com and also through the reading of such books as *Writer's Market*, which lists leading agents and editors as well as titles they have acquired. Before so much information was available on the Internet, *Writer's Market* and its competitive titles were my main source for researching the industry and getting a feel for top agents and editors.

One useful feature of such books is that they gather information from publishing houses and agents from one year and publish the book the next. In questionnaires sent to solicit information for the book, they ask to list a few specific titles which best represent the type of work that is being done. An agent, for example, will list three or four of the leading titles he or she acquired in the past year. What is interesting, though, is that at the time of information submission, the titles have not usually been published, but they will have been by the time the industry book hits the shelves. My hobby was to look up titles sold by the leading agents and match them upon release on Amazon.com to see how they were performing. Also, I would look at the titles listed by premiere publishers, figuring these are ones that they had paid large and dear advances for, and I would research these as well to determine if they were performing to expectations.

Talk to People in the Business

The very last thing someone succeeding in the publishing business as a writer, agent or editor wants is to be bothered by a hopeful writer who knows little and is merely searching for

—— oOo ——

oOo

coattails to grab onto. Personally, I get unsolicited e-mails and calls on an all-too-regular basis, and while I try to be cordial to these information seekers, it is one of the more frustrating aspects of my career. My least favorite is the one who comes seeking a recommendation to my agent or editor. If I barely know you and have never read your work, how can I suggest your work to my trusted ally?

If handled properly, however, professional contacts like myself and others can be of significant value and are undoubtedly an invaluable aspect of research by the writer-in-waiting. In my case, I was fortunate to live in a small community where the writer was a known and accessible breed, putting me within arm's reach of critical information. Tiny Oxford, Mississippi, the home of William Faulkner, is a literary hamlet where the book stands tall. As previously mentioned, long-time friend Richard Howorth owned and operated Oxford's Square Books, one of the leading independent bookstores in America. I was fortunate during the time I was doing book industry research that Howorth was serving a term as president of the American Booksellers Association. A strong-willed and strong-voiced advocate of the book, credited with timely leadership during his tenure, he was able to provide me with some general nuts and bolts of publishing in terms of reasonable expectations, places to start and areas worth focusing on. A very talented bookseller himself, I knew he could help answer questions about the merits of a proposed title. If he did not think a title had hope, how could a publishing house, which ultimately would have to convince booksellers like him to stock the book?

To be sure, almost no researching writer-to-be has a friend

oOo

─────────────────── ∘O∘ ───────────────────

and neighbor like Mr. Howorth to call on, but in every community there is a bookstore manager at Barnes and Noble or Borders or an owner or manager at a neighborhood independent store worth getting to know. After making these acquaintances, questions of merit can be proposed when the time arises. The key is to respect their time and talents and to make use of requests. They are busy, after all, with demanding jobs, and do not have time to cultivate individual relationships in most cases. Simply introduce yourself, let them know your intentions, and tell them you may approach them with industry questions occasionally. When you do, make the inquiries count. Be very specific, so that they can provide you with a focused answer.

For example, if you had a spouse who suffered from a disease such as alcoholism and were thinking you would write a book focusing on what it is like to live with a problem drinker, you could tell your bookseller about the concept and ask them if they think such a title would slot well in the stores. An experienced bookseller will likely reply with something along the lines of telling you that approach has been done several times and, that if you want to make it work, you need to find some other angle to add as a hook.

Successful writers can also be a good source for research, although be forewarned that they can be the least approachable. A full-time writer like me wants to help anybody, but the demands of deadlines and pressures to conceive of and develop new ideas makes clearing the necessary time difficult. I find that most writers prefer not to take the time to share much with one another for the simple fact that it takes too much time and energy away from issues at hand. Certainly, they like to visit and share stories

─────────────────── ∘O∘ ───────────────────

—————————— oOo ——————————

of agents and editors, but they are not as quick to talk about what they are working on and how it must come together.

A good example is someone like the bestselling non-fiction author, Michael Lewis. He and I are acquainted and have many friends in common, but we would not professionally exchange more than pleasantries because he has his work to do, and I have mine. I doubt he would appreciate me asking him for professional advice unless it was a dire situation, and I can certainly admit having the same feelings about it. His problems are his, if he has any, and mine are mine.

The truth of the matter, though, is that successful writers have valuable information to share with hopeful writers, and if you can find a way to courteously brush into their life enough for them to share some of it with you, your task of reaching and crossing over the transom will become much less difficult. A great example of this is John Grisham. I was fortunate to know America's bestselling fiction writer when he was a small-town lawyer, trying like you to launch a writing career. A nice person before his success and an even nicer person after it, Grisham's free time is far too accounted for these days to be giving out helpful hints to novices, but in the mid-1990s, I did benefit from his knowledge.

"Don't try to be me," he said. "Develop your own niche."

And that is exactly what I did, searching for and identifying an area of writing that I believed I could enter and make an impact. Admittedly, I would have loved to launch a writing career as a bestselling fiction author, becoming the next John Grisham, but the odds of that were slim. Be your own man, he was essentially telling me. Fortunately, I was smart enough to listen.

—————————— oOo ——————————

—— oOo ——

Agents are other good sources of information, but they can be more difficult to approach than writers simply because good agents are queried so often that they have little time to spend helping individuals learn the craft. It does happen, but only every once in a while, that an agent will see a unique spark or hint of rare talent in a writer, and they will take the time to answer questions and develop the writer. Remember, they just do not want phone calls or anything more than an unsolicited e-mail or letter query. Pushing for more is asking to be rejected on the spot.

The same can be said for editors. Most are overworked and can barely get through the masses of internal e-mails, much less take the time to direct a writer not under their direction by virtue of a contract. About the only time hopeful writers can get advice from agents or editors is in forums such as respected writers' conferences in which attendees are either qualified or separated by the distance of panel and audience. However, there are numerous articles written by top-level agents and editors which can be found online containing helpful tidbits and information. A few have even written books, but my experience is that the agent who has time to write a book on how to get published is not the most respected in the industry.

The bottom line, regarding agents and editors, is that they want you to do the hard work yourself, researching and asking questions of others so that by the time you reach them, you have a complete understanding of the business of writing and are ready to be productive and profitable with little hand-holding.

—— oOo ——

Chapter 2

You Can't Always
Write What You Want

Oxford, Mississippi was not your average small, Southern
town to grow up in. With just 13,000 residents and situated 50 miles south of Memphis in the relatively remote, upper
corner of the state, it would seem to be anything but a place
where diversity of ideas prospered, with far more well-educated
people than not.

In my youth, I was completely unaware of this oddity. To
me, it was just another town, and my concerns were probably
no different than those of youth in the more typical Southern
small towns — sports, the opposite sex and goofing off. Distinct differences did exist, however. Beginning in the first grade,
my down-the-street best friend was a descendent of William
Faulkner, and we often played on the grounds of Rowan Oak,

the deceased writer's estate. My friend's parents, Dean Faulkner Wells and Larry Wells, were writers themselves with an eclectic group of friends traversing through the door on a regular basis that kept life interesting.

I remember dropping by one afternoon to see my friend, only to meet a man in the living room introduced as a musician named Jimmy Buffett. I did not know about "Coconut Telegraph" at the time, recalling instead a tune that I had sung over and over two years before called "Cheeseburger in Paradise," but it was not long before I bought all of his work, becoming a 13-year-old fully versed in island music.

On another drop-by visit to my friend's house in about 1980, I remember being introduced for the first time to a writer with whom I had no familiarity. His name was Willie Morris, having just arrived back in the South from his *North Toward Home* journey. Long before the film adaptation of his book *My Dog Skip* helped a generation to know and understand more about this lovably yet complicated man, he spent his days recovering from drunken stupors of the night before. Mr. Morris' routine would also have him reemerge with friends long after the sun had gone down to laugh, jockey wittily with intellect and explore the far boundaries of conversation. He also loved a good game, but struggled to find one that made his match. I once saw him play *Trivial Pursuit*, hurling correct answers one after another despite a tongue laden with liquor. Even in a room of smart writers, his genius rose far above the crowd.

There was nothing abnormal about these seemingly odd gatherings of intellectuals to me because Oxford was a university town, after all, home to Ole Miss. My father was a

—— oOo ——

microbiologist; my friend's father a historian; another friend's mother a writer who happened to be named Faulkner. It was just a way of life, and my friends and I were far more interested in sneaking a cold beer out of the refrigerator to split or playing basketball all day or walking to the far end of town to meet a girl in her front yard rather than discussing or learning about prose.

In later years though, as if by osmosis, this atmosphere of literary and creative intellect began to rub off on me as well as on the community in which I lived. As mentioned previously, Square Books, circa 1979, was operated by Mr. Howorth. The store made quite an impact on Mr. Morris, and the writer worked to bring his close friends and big literary names to town for visits and book signing events. Some, like Barry Hannah, stayed, creating the beginning of the town's reputation as a writer's haven. Add to that the emergence of new resident John Grisham, who moved to town in 1991 as his fame was taking off internationally, and the emergence of a local fireman-turned-writer named Larry Brown, and you had the ingredients for Oxford becoming the center of the South's modern-day literary universe. Even with the passing of Larry Brown in 2004 and the moving of Grisham to Charlottesville, Virginia some years before, Oxford still today has more published writers per capita than perhaps any American city.

Think John T. Edge is the country's leading food writer or that Tom Franklin is the greatest creator of gritty fiction to come along in decades? If you spend enough time walking around Oxford's town square, you will likely run into one or both of them or any of the other published writers who call the

—— oOo ——

38655 zip code home. If that is not enough, drop into Oxford's City Hall on the square and say hello to the Mayor, the man considered by many to be one of the best booksellers of this era — Richard Howorth. For me, this atmosphere that dates back to its formation during my youth is not what led me to become a writer. It is, however, what helped make my writing career reach large-scale success. Instead of thinking small, this little town of literary greatness encouraged me to believe that anything was possible or achievable in the realm of books.

Everyone Has to Start Somewhere
My career as a writer began when I turned to journalism in college after discovering that writing stories was far easier than studying economics. Like most male student journalists, my initial exposure was through sports. I worked hard to get opportunities outside of the student newspaper, writing for a local daily paper as well as getting pay-per-story, or stringing, assignments at other papers throughout the state.

By the time I was a senior, beat jobs were offered, and I did not have to go looking because my clippings far exceeded those of others. One small daily, *The Oxford Eagle*, offered me a job with the title Assistant Sports Editor of which the experience alone was more than enough to overcome the low pay — something like $250 a week — and I seized the opportunity. My weekly column was named one of the best in the state my first year on the job, and, by the second, I had an offer to become editor of a weekly newspaper in middle Tennessee with 10 employees. There, my administrative qualities were understandably weak considering I was managing a staff as a 22-year-old, but readers

oOo

responded well to my general column, and I was recognized more for writing skills than anything else.

The work was good enough for me to land the news editor job two years later back in Oxford, and I returned to the newspaper from which I had started — this time managing the editorial general news staff. Covering and assigning stories on everything from tea parties to overgrown watermelons to breaking news of national merit, I continued writing a weekly column, which this time was of general interest, and it, too, was named one of the best in the state among newspapers of all sizes. An investigative reporting series even nabbed a regional Associated Press award. But, in taking the promotion to editor — the natural progression for someone wanting to make any money in newspapers — I found other aspects of the business were not to my liking, nor did they match up well with my talent. I was a writer, and young writers were forced to hop from metro area to metro area to gain promotion; this was a path I was not interested in taking. It seemed the only way I could advance was through management, but that was not appealing since my talents were as a columnist, not as an editor.

So I left the business in my early twenties to enter an entrepreneurial world of small business. Ranging from franchise printing and copying centers to real estate, business was not overly enjoyable with payrolls every Friday and a never-ending responsibility, but the experiences allowed me to learn valuable lessons that would come in handy later. For example, I learned that any business, no matter how large or small, must make money on a recurring basis for sustainability. No matter how good a storefront looks or how much money flows into

oOo

oOo

the top line, all that matters at the end of the day is the bottom line.

By the mid-1990s, my businesses had grown to a respectable size in sales, but I had difficulty focusing on their management because I missed writing terribly. My one true skill in the professional world — the ability to craft words in a readable style that the larger public could understand and enjoy — was not being utilized. Simply, I was missing my calling. To put my communications skills to better use, I branched out into other professional activities, like city council. I won my first term in a close, heated race against a man now considered a friend, who was more qualified than I, yet I beat him narrowly by writing all of my advertising copy myself and sending personal, well-written letters to voters in the district. Additionally, I became a vice president for one of the South's larger advertising and public relations agencies, writing everything from ad copy for clients to brand plans for businesses and municipalities.

Still, I longed to write in the purest form but could not see returning to the newspaper business with three children and many obligations. Making ends meet would not be possible. Taking note of Oxford friends like Larry Brown and John Grisham, who had launched book-writing careers from ground zero, my wife made a strong suggestion one afternoon, saying I should consider writing books for a living.

"It's perfect for you," she said.

Thinking she meant I should write novels, I disagreed.

"No, I can't do that," dropping the subject and managing to push it out of my mind for the time being.

Two years later, though, with my longing to write burning

oOo

———————————— oOo ————————————

stronger than ever before, I began to reflect on her suggestion, thinking that perhaps this was a road to the future that warranted consideration. If John Grisham, the small-town lawyer and state politician, could make millions weaving fast-moving tales; and if Larry Brown, the local-boy fireman without a college education, could make a decent living writing about his hardscrabble upbringing, then it was possible I could find an avenue fitting my abilities and make money writing about what I knew.

I kept working at my business as well as other jobs, but on the side, did what most people who think they can write a book do and started working on a memoir. My life had been marked by an unusual story that always dropped jaws when I told parts of it, and it seemed getting it into print would be a natural starting place for a new career as a writer.

The story is unusual, to say the least, and seemed the perfect intro into print. It goes something like this:

I was adopted from a Baptist children's home in New Orleans, Louisiana as an infant. My birth records were sealed, and I was only given non-identifying information about my biological mother. Legally, I could find nothing. My parents always offered to help if I ever wanted to find her, but I always kindly declined. Upon the birth of my first child, I changed my mind. For seven years I searched and looked and tried to find information by all sorts of legal and illegal means but to no avail. In desperation, I finally called someone who held the records for the state and bluffed them into getting my file. I pleaded for help. At last, he blurted out my real mother's name and her hometown and hung up the phone.

———————————— oOo ————————————

───────────────── oOo ─────────────────

She was 17 years older than me. At the time I got this information, one of my closest friends was years older than me and from the same place the man said was my birth mother's hometown. Everybody in the South is connected in some way, and I suspected odds were good that my friend knew my mother. For seven years, I had looked but turned up nothing. Then, I got a name, called up my good friend, who said, yes, he knew her.

"You look just like her," he told me.

She had been a cheerleader and a class beauty. After graduation, she disappeared. Nobody knew why. My friend promised to find her and called three days later with a married name and a new hometown. I knew the place well. And the name sounded familiar. I called my sister-in-law, who lived in large city in a neighboring state. I gave her the name.

"Oh," she said. "My gosh. That's your mother?"

It turned out that my birth mother's brother-in-law was a medical partner with my wife's brother-in-law. I had two younger half sisters and a younger half brother, none of whom knew I even existed.

As the story unfolded in the following years, with me ultimately meeting two half-sisters and one half-brother that I never knew of and who never knew they had an older brother, it only grew in jaw-dropping qualities, appearing more and more like a natural first book. I worked on the memoir in my spare time and sent several chapters to a publisher I had located once I thought they were good enough for outside eyes. My telephone rang within a week of my mailing it off to one publisher. The publisher was a small house I had chosen due

───────────────── oOo ─────────────────

oOo

to a similar title I had discovered they had published. Yes, the lady said, they were interested in my book. She was not so sure about an advance, but they wanted to publish it, which sounded fine to me.

The business of getting published seemed easy.

I continued working on the book, assuming I had a publisher and the right one at that, and began to work on the craft more at work as well, enjoying word-play at the advertising agency. Writing was fun again, and I began to recognize that this was where my true talents were. I realized very quickly that I was no Larry Brown, or John Grisham for that matter, but I also sensed that because my style was readable and I possessed a basic understanding of structure and sequence, writing books as a profession made sense. I made the decision to make a career change, telling my wife that I planned to sell the businesses and quit my job.

"Do you think you can make any money?" she asked.

"I have no idea," I replied.

And just like that, without having had a book published and not even having an agent or a book under contract, I became a full-time writer. Like long-lasting love, the career of a writer is a deliberate decision. You can talk about it and dream about it, but it will never occur unless you wholeheartedly decide that is what you are going to do without exception, embracing it and working at it with all energy. Saying that I had become a writer made me a writer.

Crazy as this may sound, I have encountered other writers who took this same path toward authorship as a career. One of my personal favorites, Lewis Nordan, writes with both beauty

oOo

and humor in his memoir *Boy With Loaded Gun* (Algonquin, 2000) about his decision to become a writer. With no credentials or credibility to his name, Nordan decided one day that he was a fiction writer, becoming obsessed with the craft to the point that all he did or talked about involved writing or writers. He had never had anything published, and in his book, he talks about having made up elaborate lies to friends about authors he knew and the types of books and short stories he was working on, but other than a colorful imagination, he had little to hang on. And because he decided without question that he was a writer, he, in fact, became a writer.

From the moment I made the decision to become a full-fledged writer, I began to think the book about my life saga that I had been toying with — the work I thought would be my natural introduction to the world of publishing — was actually just a tune-up. The manuscript needed to be shelved, if not thrown into the trash. Working on it was therapeutic at a time when I was contemplating change in life, and it was also a wonderful apprenticeship in the craft in that I had a self-produced document resembling a book which allowed me to see my own word, structural and storytelling weaknesses.

The reason I made a conclusive decision to put the project aside involved a writer's epiphany: I looked at the book as a businessman and realized that its money-making capabilities were small. My story was interesting, but other, more recognized and notable writers had written books about strange-twist adoption stories. Having an interesting story is often not enough. To write a memoir, it must be highly unusual, or involve an element of celebrity. If I became a well-read author later, the book might

∘O∘

———————— oOo ————————

make sense, but at this point, it stood to be nothing more than another small press has-been.

Just because it was the story that I wanted to write and in some ways needed to write did not mean that it was the story that was best to spend my time on trying to get published due to the business of the craft. It was a revelation that, if you want to launch a career as a successful author, you must spend your time working on and trying to get published the work that has the best chance at commercial success.

In response to this fresh thought, I immediately discarded my mostly finished manuscript about my adoption and the discovery of my birth mother and put all notions of writing out of my mind. If I wanted to earn money for my work and if I wanted a sustainable career, I needed to approach publishing just like I would any new business venture, studying and learning the ins and outs of the trade. What books were selling and what books were not? Why does an author need an agent? How does the editor relationship work? Why do some books get large advances and others do not? Why do bad books succeed and good books often do not?

The idea was that, once I learned the business of writing, I would better know what book I should be writing. Once I made the decision to become a writer, I did not need to write a single word until I understood more about the business I was entering. And that is the best advice I can give any hopeful trying to forge a career from this craft. It is fine if you want to spend your time practicing or indulging in self-therapy, working on an aimless manuscript that may not have any publishing merits. For some writers, this is enough. But, if you are like I was, aiming to make

———————— oOo ————————

— oOo —

a living and to find much commercial success, your time will be more valuably spent by putting down what you want to write and learning the business first, so that you can best determine what approach will give you a chance at launching a career.

— oOo —

Chapter 3

Find a Niche of Your Own

It has been said that everybody wants to write a book. Certainly, that is a gross exaggeration since many people in the world cannot even read a book. But from my experience as a writer, one who has been approached for trade tips from just about anybody in every walk of life imaginable, it is probably safe to say that in this country at least one out of five people wants to write a book.

It may also be presumed that the writer most would-be authors would like to emulate is one of the most commercially successful of all, legal thriller author, John Grisham. They have seen him make a transformation from small-town lawyer making moderate income to an international bestselling author bringing in millions and millions of dollars; no wonder they dream of emulating him.

oOo

Grisham's lifestyle, in the eyes of many, is perfect. He does not have to sit behind a desk all day. He has a private jet to fly him around the world, taking long stays in Paris and short excursions to Grand Cayman. When he wants to visit his daughter in college several states away, he can be there in 55 minutes. His beautiful wife always looks well-rested, and the most stress he apparently feels is making the annual deadline on a book, which he can probably write with his eyes half-closed by now. And people sit on beaches around the world by the thousands reading his books page after thrilling page.

When these millions of want-to-be writers dream of who they would like to transform into, they dream big — of becoming the next John Grisham.

This is fine for colorful imagination, but it is not too practical in terms of reality. In fact, it is about as far-fetched as a friend or family member coming to you all excited, suggesting he had a great new idea for a big business and proceeded to tell you about how he would start a fast food outlet that focused on inexpensive hamburgers, French fries and children's meals and featured big golden arches as the sign greeting arriving customers.

"You're going to start the next McDonald's?" you might ask.

I don't think this would exactly take off. It has already been done, and there is no room at the top. Subway found space in the fresh alternative area of fast-food. Taco Bell found space in the Mexican area of fast-food. But no concept has been able to dethrone McDonald's from its perch as the world's leading fast-food hamburger restaurant. Likewise, Grisham protects his well-endowed legal thriller brand by bringing out one book a year, filling available space in chain stores to capacity. Others with immense talent have tried to move into the space, but to no significant avail. John Grisham simply controls it, and he is not letting go.

That is exactly why years ago he innocently gave me some worthwhile advice: if you want to be a writer, find your own niche. Don't try to be me.

These words of wisdom were not directed at me, but were told to me in general when he was discussing in the early 1990s his fast flight to fame and fortune and during a time when many of his friends and acquaintances were suggesting they had a top-notch book in them as well.

"Let me tell you about my idea," many had insisted before falling into a babbling plot description of their sure-fire bestseller.

They had no conception, of course, that once Grisham had his breakthrough, ideas for storylines began to shower down on him like leaves falling from a tree. When I asked him in 1992, for example, when he might exhaust this plot cache, he responded smugly, "Not for a long time." Translated for the hopeful writers of the world, that means to go and find your own niche. He's got the fast-paced, legal thriller fiction area well covered.

Write What You Know, Not What You Have Lived

During the 1990s and into the early part of the turn of the century, many first-time authors introduced themselves to the publishing world with a memoir. The first-person, bare-your-soul approach was utterly en vogue during this time, and we heard from no-name writer after no-name writer, describing how they dealt with such life-altering inflictions as growing up in Alaska to living with an alcoholic father to wanting to mutilate oneself. The majority of these books were moderately successful. A few even experienced blockbuster success. But one trait most of the first-time authors share is that nobody in the writing world seems to know where they are or what they are doing now.

With rare exception, like Alice Sebold, who followed her wonderful 1999 memoir *Lucky* with a bestselling work of fiction, *The Lovely Bones,* in 2002, most of the writers who debuted with a memoir in this era have subsequently remained unpublished, unable to find a voice outside of their quirky, individualistic tales. The reason behind this is that when the memoir was red-hot, the story mattered more than the quality of writing or the author's vision for bookselling and promotion. If your father was a drunk who molested your sister, a book publishing division of Random House had a contract waiting for you.

The problem arises because, at a time when the memoir is as *out* as out can be, trying to follow such a sordid narrative with a book that appeals to the new tastes of acquiring editors proves difficult. In most cases involving these first-time authors, the memoir got them over the transom, but it turned out to be a dash inside a building with quite a shaky foundation. Once inside, they had nothing sturdy on which to stand and discovered they did not have a writing career but one book to proudly display on home and office shelves. Without a doubt, if I had followed through with my original plan of writing a memoir as my first book, my career would have met a similar fate.

It is common logic that tells us personal experience and private insight flavor writing. First-timers often take this to an extreme, however, using their life almost solely as the basis for

———————— oOo ————————

their work of fiction or non-fiction. But just because we are most comfortable writing about what we know best does not mean that every first book must give a pure reflection of our lives. In my case, a memoir of my odd adoption saga would have been nothing short of a self-portrait.

When contemplating what to write about next — after shelving my initial project — I thought my career would be best served if I used my basic knowledge to tell a story about something or someone other than myself. My objective, after all, was to become a successful, top-selling author. I should not have been so vain to assume the story had to revolve around me; there would hopefully be plenty of opportunities later in life to tell these personal stories. Perhaps, if I could narrow the field down to one in which I had more professional expertise, I would be able to find the right subject, land an agent, get a contract and write a first book successful enough to lead to another.

While studying the publishing business for a year or more and not writing a single word, I narrowed my areas of focus down to four, which seemed suitable for a first subject. The four categories consisted of those in which I not only had reasonable knowledge, but also could possibly convince an agent, then an editor, then the book buying trade and ultimately the book buying public that I held an authoritative voice.

My list was comprised of these general areas:

1) **Parenting.** As a father of three children, it seemed as logical as not that I could be an expert on the how-to aspects of rearing them. Also, as an adopted child, I thought perhaps

———————— oOo ————————

I could find a way to integrate my experiences into a more broad-based format.

2) **Sports.** My first experience as a writer involved covering sports. I still had friends who were major college coaches and finding an angle and gaining access to an interesting storyline did not seem far-fetched.

3) **Business.** I did not possess an MBA, but my years as a small business owner and as a business advertising and public relations consultant gave me unique insight into the do's and don'ts of the corporate world.

4) **Journalism.** I was not a great newspaper editor, but I did have a keen sense for writing, which turned the collective heads of the community as well as the eclectic personalities that invariably brighten and stir up a small-town newsroom.

In consideration of the options, I leaned toward fictionalizing my experiences as an employee of community newspapers. During my first job at the *Oxford Eagle*, we had a beloved photographer in the advanced stages of Alzheimer's, who could never remember to place film in her camera, and an elderly female part-owner, also serving as Editor, who made me uncomfortable when she talked about blacks, was overweight and almost blind due to diabetes. Also, I remembered encountering a sports editor at another newspaper, who could not drive because he did not know how and was forced to hitch rides to area high school football games.

My idea was to gather all of the fascinating real-life characters I had met into one newsroom, relocate them to a new small, Southern town and bring them to life in a fictional account of

oOo

a small-town newspaper, showing how insignificant stories like those about oversized tomatoes and Rotary Club meetings blend with leads of murder and unemployment. After all, if movies like *Broadcast News* could find an audience, a book about the strange personalities and stories of an American community newspaper could interest people as well.

But with circulation of daily newspapers in rapid decline, I was not sure if this generation could romanticize or connect with the oddities of piecing elements of everyday life together through the medium of ink and paper. Most people under the age of 35 that I knew did not subscribe to a newspaper. Why in the world would they want to read a book about one?

Other areas in which I had knowledge did not sound so appealing for a first book either after further review. Parenting was something I knew a bit about but so did hundreds of millions of others, from Macon, Mississippi to Sacramento, California to Beijing, China. From Dr. Spock to T. Berry Braselton, I could not imagine what I might reveal to the world that was any better or different or more invigorating about raising children. Sure, I believed that genetics matter more than environment and having children while young is better than having them when old, if given a choice. I was not convinced, however, that such wisdom was worth a dime, much less the $24.95 price of a first edition, hardcover book. With these areas excluded, the only fields of interest I had left to consider were sports and business, two subjects that ironically go hand-in-hand because of their appeal to the American middle-aged male.

As a sportswriter early in my writing career, my ability was adequate, as was my understanding of the perimeter stories,

oOo

which make the games more interesting for fans and readers. I had walked away from sports journalism though, because I never really liked the game of pandering to the personalities that held the power in each individual conference or sport. Ever try interviewing Steve Spurrier? Terrell Owens? Me neither. I did not want to stick around and try as a sportswriter, having been run off by the egomaniacs before them. Also, it is seemingly impossible to break news-worthy headlines as a sportswriter without frequently saddling up to the bar with old college and pro jocks and listening to every breath of hot air they may spew. Catering to these personalities is unfortunately part of covering the games, for better or worse, and it was an aspect I did not like, so I made a final choice to leave the business.

It was never and is not now my objective to be known solely as a writer of business books, but after breaking down a list of areas to concentrate on initially, it made much sense that my first book, or books, would focus on that genre. It was a field I had expertise in, considering that I had written brand plans for companies and communities and had run businesses of my own, having some successes but also making almost every mistake in the book at least once. The business category also seemed to be among the industry's most wide open in terms of first-time authors gaining access. As a result of the 1990s, when business publishing became a highly profitable venture, companies like Random House, Wiley and HarperCollins were on the prowl for new concepts. Typically, tried-and-true authors seemed to have a significant edge, but my year-long research revealed that first-timers were getting contracts from major houses when the

———————— oOo ————————

material was worthy and when the author had an ability to speak, promote and sell books.

The style of business book writing also fit my more recent efforts at word and document crafting. Taking complex subjects, sifting through them to find the most pertinent information, and writing it in a clear and understandable manner was a forte of mine, also fitting well with the usual format of best-selling business books. I learned from reading the quotes of pioneers in the industry such as Adrian Zackheim, now of Penguin Putnam, that the primary objective of a business book is to give the reader takeaways. It does not matter if the narrative takes a deep, detailed, journalistic approach like *Barbarians at the Gate* or if it is a short, fable-style piece like *Rich Dad, Poor Dad.* The only things readers usually want in return for their money spent on a business book are applicable lessons to use in life, at the office, or both. This was something I knew I could do, even as a first-time author. A decision was made: my first book would be a business book. All I needed to get a career started was a very good subject.

Keep Your Eyes and Ears Wide Open

It is now my opinion from some years of experience that the biggest difficulty for a hopeful writer, in their quest to get arms around what it takes to get published by a legitimate house, is to recognize what is a worthwhile story and what is not. Frequently, I am approached with ideas for new projects by readers of my books and others who know what I do for a living — and nine times out of ten, they are wayward concepts. Most people just have no idea of what will work and what will not.

———————— oOo ————————

—— oOo ——

Even for me — a writer who has sold eight concepts to contract in less than four years, some off nothing more than a few lines in an e-mail, and who has been told by some of the leading agents, editors and executives in the publishing business that his ideas are a strong point — finding the perfect subject and then developing the right slant on it can be difficult. At the time of publication of this book, I had signed eight contracts to write books worth more than $500,000 in advances, but I had tried to sell 11 concepts through my agent — meaning three failed. Honestly, I felt two of the three that did not grab sufficient interest to advance to contract stage were extremely worthy projects with best-selling potential. The proposals looked strong. The story lines were compelling, and the subjects held international appeal, yet no editors took the bait, leaving the projects lifeless.

In the very beginning, though, I believed my first idea was a sure-fire winner. It came to me in part through hard work, which put me in a position to get the opportunity, and part through raw luck. But after a year of studying the business of publishing and another nine months or so doodling with ideas for my first proposal to pitch to an agent, I knew my career as a writer was on the verge of launching.

How the subject came to be is this:

I was still living in my hometown, Oxford, when an announcement was made that Mississippi would land its first automaker, Nissan. The Japanese company, which was headed by a colorful, emerging executive named Carlos Ghosn, had chosen the state as the site of its new North American manufacturing facility. Shortly after the announcement, Ghosn was

—— oOo ——

———————— °O° ————————

making a trip from Japan to the United States and wanted to tour the entire state of Mississippi to get a feel for the area in which his company was to be conducting future business. A stop of his trip, naturally, would be Oxford, the hamlet of the state. A dear friend and professional colleague of mine was asked to be Mr. Ghosn's tour guide for the northern portion of his visit. Recognizing my interest in international business and my ability to discuss an array of subjects due to a journalist's knowing "a little bit about a lot of things," she invited me to co-host Nissan's chief executive, joining him for lunch and a driving tour.

From the moment I met Carlos Ghosn, we had a kinship. I admired his direct style and immense intellect, and he seemed to like the honesty with which I answered his questions. Over lunch, he posed a question to the table, inquiring why none of us drove a Nissan. One guest gushed on about how great the products were, stating that he never bought one because, well, he wasn't sure why. I looked Mr. Ghosn in the face and told him the truth, that Nissan at the time had no products I would ever consider buying. The product lineup was limited to entry-level vehicles like the Sentra sedan and a small pickup truck, and the Maxima, while excellent, was not quite my style. Mr. Ghosn was well aware at the time of his taking over Nissan that the company was product starved, and this was one reason for the company's severe struggles. My answer was honest and correct, and he appreciated my candor. The relationship built successfully from there.

Mr. Ghosn shook hands with me at his departure and gave me a business card with his personal contact information in

———————— °O° ————————

———————————————— oOo ————————————————

Japan, saying that if I ever had anything that would help him in his job, to send it along. I did not contact him immediately about a book because I felt like it would be too forthright. Instead, I began to study his career as a hobby, learning with fascination how dramatic a turnaround he was engineering at Nissan — a Westerner, Mr. Ghosn is a Brazilian-born man of Lebanese descent, who speaks five languages fluently, leading a Japanese company through reform. I also took two opportunities to share with him what seemed to be useful information. For example, a stockbroker living along the Mississippi Gulf Coast had told me about a trend in which customers were seeking Nissan bonds after the announcement of the plant. I passed this word along to Mr. Ghosn, suggesting that their public relations efforts were working well. He apparently appreciated this information.

Once I believed I had a comfortable grasp on his direction and accomplishments at Nissan, the time felt right to approach Mr. Ghosn about doing the first-ever English book about his leadership. Already, he had a bestselling book co-authored by himself in Japan, but he had purposefully limited translation rights for it, keeping a lid, so to speak, on his captivating story. By telling his story from a third-person point of view and penning the book in the U.S., I believed Nissan and Mr. Ghosn would benefit from the additional publicity, and I would have an unbelievable hook on a first book project. In business terms, it is called a "win-win" situation. I pitched the concept to Nissan, and eventually Mr. Ghosn and I met to discuss it, this time on a trip of his to Detroit, and we both agreed it was a project worth doing. He asked me what I needed, and I said complete

———————————————— oOo ————————————————

———————————— oOo ————————————

access. Mr. Ghosn agreed and even went further by allowing me to do the book with no strings attached—whatever the real story was, I would be able to tell it however I saw fit.

Certainly, I experienced an element of luck in meeting Mr. Ghosn at the time I was considering a career as a full-time author, but part of my success was in my ability to recognize the story. Easily, I could have passed the idea off when realizing that Mr. Ghosn had already written a book in his own words. Just as easily, I could have considered that a Mississippi man had no business writing about a multicultural leader transforming a Japanese automaker. But knowing Mr. Ghosn personally and understanding his hard-nosed, calculated style as well as grasping the strengths of his turnaround tactics, the value of this project became more and more obvious.

I had worked to narrow down my field of initial writing to business, and I had kept my eyes open for months, looking for the right opportunity. And that is the challenge for every want-to-be writer. To find the right story, you have got to determine what you know and can write about most effectively since, often, your first shot out of the author's gate must be your best if sustainability is a goal. Then, you must look around and listen, seeking angles and avenues where you have particular knowledge or insight. Finally, when the pieces seem to fit, it is time to pull the trigger, deciding on a subject and approaching it with vigor, ready to prove to the publishing world first and to the reading world next that the story you have to tell matters.

———————————— oOo ————————————

Chapter 4

The Agent Relationship

The question most writers in search of a career ask is whether or not they need an agent in the first place? Usually, they hope that they do not, finding the frequently closed doors, occasional haughty attitudes and extensive frustration to be a complete turn off to the business. The reality is that while it is completely possible for authors to represent themselves and land a lucrative contract, it is highly unusual and also unlikely. If a no-name hopeful wants to become a known-name writer, an agent is often the key that opens the door, bringing the transom in full view, ready for crossing.

The reasons an agent is imperative to the publishing industry and, therefore, your writing career are numerous, but at the top of the list is the fact that in an industry that relies

—————————————— oOo ——————————————

on seclusion, they are the filter that reduces the clutter and wasted time, narrowing down the field of submitted queries and manuscripts to those that matter. It is true that agents may pose a serious annoyance to publishers trying to strike a deal on a book they want, always pushing for higher advances and more liberal contract terms. Rarely is the agent beholden to any one publisher, shopping instead for the best terms, and many a friendship has been lost in the industry when a deal was yanked away at the last minute so that a higher bidder could have the project.

Still, for all of the pains and complaints editors and publishers have had with agents through the years, they do not want to see literary representation vanish because it would remove the one shield they have from the hundreds of thousands of unqualified people in the world, who think they can write the next, big bestseller. For proof of this fact, I recall a statement from HarperCollins Publisher and chief executive Jane Friedman, an acquaintance I consider among the best and most influential leaders in the entire global publishing business. During a C-Span interview with her a couple of years ago that I was fortunate to catch in entirety, Ms. Friedman stated clearly that agents were a necessity in the business, searching through masses of material so that only credible proposals were submitted to publishers for consideration. From these worthy proposals, only a handful are selected and given life with a small chance of flourishing.

In agents, editors and publishers typically find a few contacts they trust and refuse to work with many they do not. They quickly learn those who bring forth the highest quality of submissions and who play fairly and respond to these agents

—————————————— oOo ——————————————

immediately, seeking their proposals sooner rather than later. Therefore, searching out an agent proves a necessary step toward getting published. And, furthermore, forging a relationship with one of the best is of the utmost importance if your quest is to command six-figure advances and deliver proposals that editors will take note of and read at once, not three weeks later.

Of the hundreds of literary agents working full-time in the publishing industry in this country, it is my experienced guess that probably not more than 250 are worth associating with. I know that makes for challenging odds in finding representation, and this issue alone can be enough to curb the hopefulness in any aspiring writer's quest, but that is the harsh reality of this business. Many people try to pass themselves off as literary agents, but the number remains relatively small of those who talk daily with leading editors and who execute deals on a regular basis. And it is this tier of top agents who you must identify through your research and with whom you must forge a professional relationship, if your career is to take root and flourish.

Make a List of Agents to Query

It may be said that the book publishing industry follows a cobbled road of queries. Editors are queried by agents with book concepts to see if they will accept a full proposal or manuscript to consider, and agents are queried by authors as to whether or not their book ideas are legitimate and deserving of a representation agreement. As for the initial stage, much has been written about how want-to-be writers should approach agents, offering specific guidelines posed as absolutes for the process. My experience, however, is that how you approach the agent

oOo

does not matter nearly as much as the quality of the project or your ability to write and sell books. I had read, for example, that agents will not accept sloppy, handwritten letters or e-mail attachments of any kind but found both of those threads of advice to be false.

A major portion of my research on the business of publishing focused on agents since I had been told of their importance to the writer. I wanted to know which ones were knocking down multiple as well as significant contracts in real-time — not five or 10 years before. From this research, I came up with a list of five that I thought would be a good representative match for me, judging from the types of titles each had recently sold, whether or not they had a website (this is the 21st century, although many agents like to think otherwise) and whether they were considered in non-fiction to be among the top handful in the country. Some writers feel uncomfortable querying multiple agents at once, and I have seen where some advice books even suggest avoiding it. But my conflicting perspective was that agents submit to editors in multiples all the time, so it hardly seemed fair to have to approach them one at a time while they slogged through piles of mail, searching for time to review your submission. Get a good list and approach this handful all at once.

When crafting your query letter, heed my advice: make it as clear and concise as possible. Agents are immediately turned off by rambling queries in which the writer works too hard to qualify his or her strengths. There is plenty of time to show later why you are the perfect writer for the project, but in the beginning, your aim is simply to grab attention so that you gain the opportunity to make a full pitch later. Many books focused specifically on

oOo

———————————— oOo ————————————

writing proposals and queries have examples of successful letters, but my suggestion is to abide by the three-paragraph maximum rule, punching your leading points emphatically and not worrying about lack of depth. For example, if I decided at this very moment that I wanted to query an agent with a pitch for a book about my adoption story, I likely would use this approach:

Dear Agent's Name,

No man has ever completely bared his soul in print about the heartache of living as an unwanted bastard child. My book will be the first, however, and I am looking for an agent to represent it in the trade.

A Bastard's Life will tell the story of how I struggled as a teenager with the issue of being given away, and how I decided as an adult I wanted to find my roots. The book will detail specifics of how I searched for my biological mother and ultimately found her, taking the reader along the emotional roller coaster ride that followed as we later met and tried to forge a relationship.

I think you will find that my proposal is strong, and, therefore, I hope you will take a long look at it and consider representing it.

Best,

David Magee

For the Carlos Ghosn book, I took a similar approach, developing a short and simple query that stated I was prepared to write the book about one of the best business stories of our time. Among those on my initial list were Frank Weimann of

———————————— oOo ————————————

oOo

The Literary Group www.theliterarygroup.com and Elizabeth Frost-Knappman of New England Publishing Associates www .nepa.com. I queried three by mail, hand-addressing the envelopes with my left-hand scrawl so that my letters stood out in the pile of others, and two by e-mail, taking advantage of the direct entries of those who listed personal e-mail addresses on their web site.

These latter two had an automatic advantage if they wanted me since I have little patience for snail mail, preferring instead the instant action and responses of electronic messages. Both agents responded within 24 hours, requesting a full proposal, while the other three contacted me by mail within the week with the same request, meaning that my initial agent query of my book project on Carlos Ghosn got a very warm reception. Also, I had come across another agent named Peter Rubie www.prlit.com on the Internet, who had written a book for *Writer's Digest* titled *Writer's Market FAQs*. If he wrote a book on publishing and also served as an agent, I figured he had the necessary tools to represent an author. So, even though he was not on my original list, I queried him by e-mail as well. When he responded favorably, another proposal was immediately dropped off in the chain of mail by the next day.

The material that I sent these agents broke a few so-called industry rules as well. Good proposals are supposed to be 50 or more pages if the author is a first-timer since editors will not convince publishers to spend money on someone they are not sure has the ability to actually develop a concept into a full-length manuscript. Ideally, the perfect non-fiction proposal will contain an overview, an author bio, a marketing plan outline, a

oOo

———————————— oOo ————————————

competitive titles section, a chapter-by-chapter description, and at least two completed sample chapters. I took the abbreviated approach, however, sending in initially a 25-page proposal that contained one sample chapter. I was certainly not opposed to preparing and sending in more pages, but I believed with all of my heart that the proposal I had developed (see *Appendix A*) was already very strong and that watering it down with more might actually achieve less.

The strength of this proposal, or any proposal, for that matter, was a crisp overview of several pages that easily framed the subject and approach of the book. Also, I spent a lot of time developing chapter headings that were action-oriented and compelling. To this day, I believe the table of contents is one of the key elements of a book proposal because both editors and marketing personnel look closely to see if the outline comes to life. Often, would-be writers will simply use broad phrases as chapter headings, and the proposal will typically fall flat during initial glances. A business book proposal, for example, about a company that experienced a turnaround will be better served with a chapter titled, *The Art of Changing Persons*, as opposed to one titled, *Analyzing Personnel*.

With my first, relatively well-developed proposal in deployment, the first to respond after receiving it was Ms. Frost-Knappman, who said the work was quite sellable but indicated it would not be marketable without one additional sample chapter. The second to respond was Mr. Weimann, who said the proposal had its strengths, but due to its short nature and my anonymity, it would have to be longer for him to consider. With the same advice from both, I added a second chapter and resubmitted the

———————————— oOo ————————————

—————————————— oOo ——————————————

proposal. Mr. Weimann responded by mail roughly one week later, writing that due to his full client lineup, he was simply too busy to adequately represent the work. However, Ms. Frost-Knappman had responded by e-mail within three days that she would love to represent the proposal, attaching an agency contract along with it for me to print and sign.

Two of the others who had received my proposal responded two weeks later that they would like to represent it. Of course, this was long after I had agreed to work with Ms. Frost-Knappman and after the last of the original five passed, like Mr. Weimann. The lone non-responder was Mr. Rubie until I finally contacted him again by e-mail with an inquiry as to whether he had received it, and he shot back a rather rude response, suggesting he did not have time to read the proposal which he had requested. In hindsight, I realized that his request to see the proposal was accompanied with a form e-mail letter recommending his book on writing. Odder yet was a form rejection letter Mr. Rubie's office sent to me some nine months later, long after I had accepted a six-figure contract for the book and had time to finish the entire manuscript. In essence, he was rejecting what in theory could have been one of the largest deals he had ever done, just as the book was about to reach bookstore shelves. His letter is proof that agents, like editors, do not always know a good concept when they see it, and it serves as a wonderful, personal novelty that I keep to show hopeful writers that they should not take rejection too harshly. Often, agents get too busy and do not even read requested materials, rejecting them for the sake of clearing the clutter from the office.

—————————————— oOo ——————————————

————— oOo —————

As it worked out for me, I gained the services of an excellent agent and a wonderful person when I signed with Ms. Frost Knappman. She and her husband, Ed Knappman, are highly respected within the industry and have years of experience with editors and publishers to serve as support. Within days of my signing the agency contract, she had my proposal out to 10 or so editors for review and was fielding calls and e-mails, explaining the merits of the project. Despite the robust response, a deal was not made immediately because the proposal was sent out around mid-December, just about the time many acquiring editors and publishers leave the office for two or more weeks for the holidays. As any agent will tell you, the worst time to sell a book is just before Christmas.

Consequently, the best time to sell a project may be the first of the year, when the powers-that-be in publishing return for the new year, needing to find projects for another season and wanting to work hard to make up for the extensive time off. By mid-January, I had received personal calls inquiring about the project from Penguin Putnam Portfolio division publisher Adrian Zackheim, former HarperCollins executive editor David Conti, Wiley's Matthew Holt, and McGraw-Hill's Jeffrey Krames. Because my agent believed I could answer their inquiries directly as opposed to her serving as a middle man of sorts, she led them directly to me, a fortunate move that allowed for some key relationships to develop. Ultimately, HarperCollins made the best offer—an advance above $100,000, significant for a first time non-fiction author—and that is who we chose to make a deal with. The next deal I made, however, was with Mr. Holt, and to this day I have a wonderful relationship with Mr. Zackheim.

————— oOo —————

———————————————————— oOo ————————————————————

Despite a very good deal and my admiration and professional respect for Ms. Frost-Knappman, I realized that I was perhaps not a good fit for her as a client from an ideological point of view. I am a goal-oriented, success-driven person, who sets high objectives and works to achieve them. She saw some of this as youthful naivety, I strongly suspected, spending much of her time trying to sober me with what she saw as the harsh reality of publishing. Without a doubt, she had much wisdom to offer, but I recognized that I needed someone to serve not in a parental role, but in a more supportive role. She brokered a second deal for me, another $100,000 advance, but it was one that I essentially pulled together on my own, battling wills all along the way of how it should be done. Right or wrong, I wanted freedom to do business my way, so we professionally parted ways, though I have been quick to recommend her services and will continue to do so because her representation was excellent.

How I ended up with my next literary agent afterward is a story worth recounting because it shows that rejection in this business is not always permanent. What does not seem to make sense to an agent or editor one minute often does in hindsight, and that was my experience with Frank Weimann of The Literary Group. The agent of such bestselling authors as Homer Hickman and Terry Bradshaw, Weimann found intrigue in my never-say-never approach in which I did not let his rejection turn me away. I never tried to bother him, but I walked a fine line considering he did not represent me. When my first deal was made, I sent him an e-mail announcing it, a kind of, "See, you could have had 15 percent of this type of thing." Then, I closed with something along the lines of, "I'm an author worth watching," hoping he

———————————————————— oOo ————————————————————

—————————————— ∘O∘ ——————————————

would eventually change his mind since I felt like his personality and approach were more to my suiting than others.

Well, Mr. Weimann was watching after all, paying attention all along the way as I pinged his inbox with infrequent messages about deals I had done or New York restaurants I had eaten in, reminders that David Magee was not going away. When I had officially parted ways with my original agent, I sent Mr. Weimann a proposal I had done called *The Greatest Fight Ever*, about the impossibly long, epic bare-knuckle match of the late 1800s between John L. Sullivan and Jake Kilrain. Within minutes, he e-mailed me back after glancing at the attachment to say he wanted to sign me up as a client of his at The Literary Group. My persistence had paid off. Two years after I had first contacted him, Mr. Weimann was selling a project as my agent.

We got several bites and one significant suitor on my boxing book proposal, but the money discussed was not nearly enough. When Mr. Weimann called to suggest we move along to another project, he told me his side of the story of how I came to be a client. "Boxing," he said, "never sells." He jumped at the proposal, however, because he realized he had made a mistake the first time and did not want to let me get away as a client a second time.

"You've got talent," he said. "I made that mistake once. I wasn't going to make it twice."

As of publication of this book, we have since done four deals together.

How It Works

Literary agents are not unlike other sales agents: sometimes, they work awfully hard for a deal and don't get paid nearly enough;

—————————————— ∘O∘ ——————————————

—————————————— oOo ——————————————

other times, big deals fall in their lap, and they get paid a large sum of money for seemingly little effort at all.

In my situation, my very first deal was the only one that the agent did top to bottom with no input from myself. But as a hands-on negotiator who forges strong editor relationships, I essentially designed each of the next seven deals for the rights to my work, yet nearly every one has to be "cleared" and negotiated in the final stages by an agent. Some people might assume that I am a fool, considering that the standard fee charged by an agent is 15 percent. To date, my agents have earned more than $75,000 despite most of the deals having been done by me. But there is more to this subject than meets the eye.

First of all, John Grisham can get a deal by himself with any publisher in the world, earns millions of dollars and happens to be a lawyer himself, well equipped to handle negotiations, yet he still uses an agent. The same can be said about Stephen King, who after writing dozens of books could easily call up his publisher himself and cut a deal, but he still uses an agent. Likely, these gentlemen have crafted a deal with their agents paying less than 15 percent commission, which makes sense when earnings are in the significant seven figure range. The point, however, is that when given a choice, they opted for literary representation.

In my case, Mr. Weimann has not only made important suggestions about the finer points of contracts he has overseen, but he is also a valued professional advisor, who helps me weigh strengths and weaknesses of projects and proposals. Additionally, he has brought me work in the form of business contacts with other clients, usually celebrities, who need a co-author,

—————————————— oOo ——————————————

as well as lending me more clout as an author because of my association with a top-name agent. Beyond all of those services, agents still do more for writers in earning their standard 15 percent commission of all advances, royalties and fees. Most importantly, they oversee publishers' accounting on disbursements, make prodding collection calls to publishers running behind on scheduled payments, and secure additional rights for authors when possible.

On at least two different occasions that I recall, editors have suggested to me that since I could make my own contract deal, I could let my agent go, but I resisted, figuring the savings of 15 percent commission in the short run would harm me in long-term goals. Recently, I had a sense of validation when I was approached by another agent seeking a co-writer for what I will call a very big business book. It was obvious to me, in checking this opportunity out, that I could potentially be involved in one of the bigger business books of this decade. I could have rather easily worked out the general terms of how my deal with the primary author would work, but the many finer points in between could conceivably add up to thousands of unearned dollars if not properly outlined in writing. Therefore, I simply turned the negotiation over to Mr. Weimann, who within three days brought me back a fair and satisfactory deal. Also, when the day comes—and it will—that I want to seek advances outside of my normative range, it will take his skills to negotiate a deal with a publisher.

Since I need his representation to further my writing career and he needs writers like me to generate commissions and pay the bills, we work together to provide enough help and support

oOo

to get the job done, and we also try not to spend useless time meeting, talking on the phone or e-mailing. It is a fine line between service and solitude that allows the agent-author relationship to flourish. If I dial up my agent on the telephone, he knows I am going to say or ask something important. If I send him an e-mail, he knows it is worth reading because I respect his business too much to clog his inbox with copies of peripheral information scraps. Conversely, if he calls me, I know I should answer, and if he sends an unsolicited e-mail, it is the first one I read.

However, beyond this basic communication, snippets of small talk are rare, and I almost never use him as a source for my continuing research and education on the publishing industry. It is not that I don't like him—I do, very much. But people working in publishing have fears and phobias about being smothered, and if you try to move too far into their space, they will recoil, shutting you out, commissions be damned. A writer who pushes an agent too far runs the risk of having a representative who is barely working on their behalf, if at all. So I try to keep communications brief and focused squarely on the business at hand. In return, he dotes on me and probably other clients not with fluffy small-talk, but by sending me large royalty checks paid to him on my behalf by overnight, express delivery.

When I have shared this payment information with other authors represented by other agents, they can barely believe it. I, too, will admit frustration waiting for almost 30 days from a previous agency for payment. The reason most agents hold checks for a period of time—and it is completely logical—is so their payment from the publisher can safely clear the bank before they

oOo

issue a check from their own account. Still, I have immensely enjoyed the perk of having the large checks sent overnight.

Equally, I have enjoyed the overall relationship with my agents because, as an author, I recognize that the benefits far outweigh the disadvantages. My experience has been that most other authors feel the very same way. It is just the work of getting to the point of representation that causes so many headaches, from repeated rejections to non-responses to haughty attitudes. The good news, however, is that if a writer-to-be does the research required to identify agents that will be the best fit, sends them a proposal on a worthy subject, and shows them an enthusiastic but non-obtrusive face, the odds of landing a quality agent will rise dramatically. Then, it is just a matter of learning what styles of communication work best for both and remembering that the object is not to gain constant attention, but to obtain fair and well-paying contracts that allow you to live your dream, writing for a living.

Chapter 5

Dealing with an Editor

The biggest eye-opener in publishing for me has been recognizing the role of the editor in today's industry. With the exception of some, like Algonquin's Shannon Ravenel or a handful at Knopf, most editors today spend very little, if any, actual time working with an author on how to craft and improve their manuscript. Most often, editors at the larger publishing houses are charged with title acquisition and contributing to the quarterly profit margin, not line-by-line editing of a submitted text.

The typical editor is required to bring in anywhere from 10 to 25 new titles per year and has a significant approval role in everything from cover and copy design to marketing plans. Each of these titles must be managed to make sure manuscripts

oOo

arrive on time and at least meet the expectations of concept and quality for which they were acquired. This management also ensures advance checks are processed properly and accurate sales forecasts have been made. Once these titles have been published, they join a long list of back titles that have to be managed as well, determining whether and when paperback editions should be released. Add to this the never-ending duties of scouring for new titles and attending acquisitions and internal protocol meetings and you can see why most editors cannot sit down for weeks imagining how manuscripts should be rewritten or improved.

My perspective on the role of the editor is a bit unique since I not only work with them as an author but have become one myself. Stemming partly from my intrigue with the publishing industry, which grew during my research of the business, and partly from an entrepreneurial passion, I started my own niche publishing company in 2002. Founded in Oxford and now located in the Chattanooga, Tennessee area, Jefferson Press www.jeffersonpress.com, the publisher of this book, is a small house that focuses on bringing titles to life of national interest and importance. We have published some wonderful titles, such as *Traveling Literary America* by B.J. Welborn and a reprint of Will Campbell's noted memoir *Forty Acres and a Goat*. My role as publisher of the company is to oversee all aspects of the business. Jefferson Press is now fortunate to have an acquisitions editor, among other employees, but in the beginning, with nobody else, the role was mine.

It was my job to negotiate contracts, talk about projects with authors and counsel them through the editorial process. Even

oOo

oOo

now, I still keep periodic dialogue with the authors when larger issues arise, and it is a position that I enjoy because it allows me to see the business from the other side. While I continue writing books of my own for other publishing houses, I am not as apt to fire off dim-witted questions to my editors or bother them unnecessarily when I get doses of such myself. I have also learned that there are really just two things an editor wants from an author: to deliver a manuscript of promised quality on time and to help sell a surprising amount of books. When these criteria are not met, books disappoint, and all the little communications concerning lesser-meaning issues can become a nag.

What authors have to understand is that, even at a small publishing company like Jefferson Press, most acquiring editors do not have the power or authority to make deals on their own. To contract a new book, most have to prepare well-crafted outlines as to why a book can succeed, make budget projections, and present the information before at least one, and usually two, committee meetings where fellow workers try to punch holes in the validity of a project. If the editor and the publisher love the book, yet the director of sales and marketing has a funny feeling, it will be no-can-do, with the editor calling the author's agent to break the news that the book will not fly. On several occasions, I have had an editor get excited about a project only to be brought down by the expectations of co-workers. Conversely, I once talked to an editor who was lukewarm on a project but took it to a publisher who absolutely loved it, suggesting the company place a higher bid. The point I am making with this workplace scenario is that, to bring in a book, editors typically have to promise their soul and convince all on the publisher's

oOo

———————— oOo ————————

editorial committee that it will work—make money. In the end, this is the bottom line and what they most want to see happen. The scenario reminds me of a conversation I had once with an author of Jefferson Press. Attempting to explain why we were no longer spending money to promote their title, I sent the author an e-mail listing all the reasons, including the fact that reviews had not been as strong as we had hoped, and because of this, there was little we could do. The author responded with a valid question.

"I thought you loved my book?"

"I did," I told the author, "but that was before it only sold 1,500 copies."

Never Bite the Hand That Feeds You

My first significant relationship with an editor was with David Conti of HarperCollins, who acquired my first book. Though he is no longer with the company, Mr. Conti was particularly skilled on the editorial side of publishing and had advanced in his career under Adrian Zackheim, who was directing the business division at HarperCollins. Mr. Zackheim is a big-thinking, marketing wizard type, who stands as a pillar in the business of publishing and is known for his creative thinking and ability to get books into readers' hands. For him, Mr. Conti was a wonderful ally and represented the editorial strength of the department. But when Penguin Putnam lured Mr. Zackheim away from HarperCollins in 2002, it left Mr. Conti with new leadership to work with and the needed synergy never occurred, so he left the company at the end of 2003. It was my privilege to be one of the last few authors to work directly with Mr. Conti

———————— oOo ————————

——————————— oOo ———————————

at HarperCollins on a project that he acquired and completely oversaw, and while I will be the first to say that he seemed overworked and overstressed during our relationship, he remained the consummate professional throughout, giving me a wonderful introduction to the agent-editor experience.

The lessons learned were many, but among the most significant was that an editor's time is precious, far more so than an agent's, and it should be treated with due care. As noted previously, most agents only like the telephone to ring when the call involves a matter of concern and much merit. Most editors are even more persnickety, for obvious reasons. They not only get unsolicited calls and e-mails from hopeful writers off the street, who cleverly find contact information, but they also have to manage dozens of authors, dozens of agents, employees working under them, and often corporate red tape that binds them from the top.

With Mr. Conti, I recall only calling him on the telephone twice, once at his suggestion and the other at mine. Both times we talked on the telephone, I remember him having to get off to make a scheduled meeting. E-mail was the preferred method of communication because it is quick, concise and clear.

"When do you anticipate having the first half of the manuscript completed?" he asked.

"Next week," I responded.

"Great, thanks. I'll read it over the weekend and get back to you," he said.

It was as simple as that. I e-mailed the first half of my first manuscript, and he did as he said, reading it over a weekend, e-mailing me back minor changes to consider before moving

——————————— oOo ———————————

—— oOo ——

forward. He did not tell me how to repair the weak spots; he only pointed them out as a matter of distinction. When other issues came up, like the completion of a cover design, he e-mailed the artwork to me along with a functional question.

"Do you like it?"

If I had wanted more attention—I did not—I could have asked, but the point of the author-editor relationship is to craft a book that has a chance of becoming a bestseller. These days, big publishers do not care about having a mid-list success, a book that sells anywhere from 5,000 to 25,000 units. They want homeruns, books that can impact bottom lines with $500,000 or more. And for a book to have any shot at this, many pieces have to come together in the early stages of development. Therefore, it is best to be in good graces with your editor, since they oversee or approve the aspects that matter most. In the courtship process—when the agent is selling a manuscript to a publisher—the editor is naturally wooing the author. But once the ink on the contract is dry and the manuscript reaches the development stage, it is the author who needs to do the wooing, helping the editor understand at every turn how strong their book is without overstepping the bounds of professional pushiness and discomfort. Also, the pain-in-the-backside author stands little chance of having his or her editor execute an option on another book.

At Wiley, my second publishing company to work with, and under the leadership of Senior Editor Matthew Holt, I found a more author-friendly house that spent more time seeking input and approval. Perhaps, this was because Mr. Holt and I were good teammates, working well together. I liked his hunger, and

—— oOo ——

oOo

he liked mine. Plus, we found ourselves stuck together for hours on end, including one time in Manhattan when the lights went out on the entire city during the blackout of 2003.

We had just eaten a great lunch at a popular Cuban restaurant in Hoboken, N.J. and were walking to the subway to catch a train back into the city when the lights went out in the station moments before we would climb aboard. Before anyone realized the electricity was out all over the Northeast, including all of the New York City metropolitan area, we found a cab, which took us across the river and back into Manhattan until a paralyzing traffic jam forced us to get out and walk. Mr. Holt and I spent hours on end together that afternoon, walking aimlessly and talking about the ins and outs of publishing. It was a crash course in the business from his perspective, which proved wonderfully helpful to me. Eventually, we realized the lights were not coming back on, and we took off walking—he, a nine-hour stroll to get home and me, coming with him for those nine plus another hour to my hotel.

From this visit, a friendship emerged that continues to this day, but it is important to note that it never discolored our professional relationship. He still crunched me, hard, when we negotiated a new contract for another book, and he still got annoyed if I got too happy with the send button on my e-mail account. I remember asking why he had not responded to one message that was quite important, and he replied with a terse note.

"David…so many e-mails from you, how can I remember?"

We both laughed about it later, because he was unquestionably right in his point. In friendship, I had perhaps drifted from the hard stance I take regarding e-mails to agents and editors,

oOo

oOo

finding myself in a red-faced moment. Instead of being defensive, I cut back on the number of e-mails sent to Mr. Holt, and we continue a wonderful relationship to this day. Since I currently have no books under contract with him, he is often a great industry source for me, answering questions, and on occasion I have been able to return the favor, helping him with issues and questions from a writer's perspective. Recently, I got an outstanding referral from him that resulted in a lucrative co-writer's contract, and I keep an eye out for any ideas to send along that fit into his publishing realm.

Such a relationship is apparently unusual, since experience tells me that more times than not, authors end up frustrated with their editor. The business is difficult, and most books fall short of expectations, leaving both parties sensitive and edgy. This happened once concerning Mr. Holt and me when a book we were particularly excited about was poised to break out, but one anticipated area of support failed to develop. He was looking for a big number to boost the company's end-of-year margins, and I was looking for a large royalty check, but neither materialized. For three or four weeks, our conversations were short, if not terse, but I worked to make sure trust and respect remained, as did he. We both recognized that disappointment was part of publishing, keeping above-board communication intact. It was a wise decision, to say the least, and I strongly suspect that in the coming years we will work together on a project again.

When Duty Calls

Several months after signing my first contract with Harper-Collins, I ran into a well-read and educated friend on the street,

oOo

oOo

who inquired about my developing manuscript. It was coming along okay, I told him, but there were rough spots.

"Oh, well," he responded. "HarperCollins will help you get it right."

His statement could not have been farther from the truth. While Mr. Conti did read my manuscript upon its submission and put forth helpful suggestions, the reality is that large publishing houses do not write or rewrite manuscripts for authors. First of all, the liability would be too great if editors actually wrote manuscripts in the names of others. There is a fine line between helping an author point out weaknesses and doctoring their work.

When publishing companies distribute a book, the copyright is just about always held in the name of the author on the premise that it is their work. The publisher is merely licensing the right to print and sell the work. Second, as noted previously in this chapter, editors at big houses just do not have the time to be writers, too. If they did, many would simply be writing books of their own instead of working 70-hour weeks and dealing with Manhattan commutes.

Of the five editors I have worked with thus far, I suspect that only two actually read my finished work cover to cover. It sounds like an outrageous statement, I know, but it never raised my eyebrows or blood pressure. Others inside the companies, like the publisher or members of the marketing team, read the books and got excited about their potential, so that was enough for me. I will admit my surprise when I first learned that editing at large publishing houses usually means nothing more than a couple of trips through a copyeditor's hands. None of my research of

oOo

—————————— oOo ——————————

the business revealed that editors rarely edit anymore, but the oversight was purely my fault. I had rightly concluded, after all, that big-time publishing was a big business, facing demands of having to reach higher and higher profits with less and less staffing. Editors, like the rest of us in the business the world, can only do so much.

The realization of this fact can perhaps help want-to-be writers better understand the difficult maze of protocol and submissions they are forced to traverse in trying to reach and cross over the transom. By forcing hopefuls to put all ideas down in writing, first in the form of a query and then in the form of a proposal, the publishing world effectively gains assurance that once a writer reaches the contract stage for the first time, they actually have the ability to deliver a formidable manuscript. This selective reduction process allows the editor to focus on more clerical items, such as deadlines, promotional copy and sales meetings.

This is not to suggest that real editing no longer occurs. At smaller publishing companies, this is often the norm. Jefferson Press editor Henry Oehmig works closely with authors to make sure the story they are writing is worthy of publication. He does not do the work for them, but reaches beyond the advice that is provided by editors at many larger houses, emphasizing literary structure and endorsing a view of publishing that believes book buyers are paying for more than just words. With few exceptions, it is the small houses who labor to make a book a complete package, with cover and interior design and thorough editing standing as equal parts in this.

A good example of this dedication to shaping good books focuses on a first-time author we recently acquired who had an

—————————— oOo ——————————

oOo

excellent concept, a head-turning marketing scheme, and some crafty sentences to offer. The author did not, however, have a completed manuscript that was book-worthy. That is why, despite having a solid package to sell in the hands of a credible agent, the book slipped through the cracks of larger publishers into our hands. There was no reason for them to acquire a product with editorial flaws, requiring extensive time and work to correct when literally hundreds of other projects could more easily slip into the slot. But for Jefferson Press, the work will prove worthwhile if the author responds well to the editorial suggestions, ending up with an excellent manuscript to go along with a solid marketing plan and a wonderful subject concept.

In 2005, I signed for the first time with a publishing house that would be considered a small press and have found it to be a gratifying experience working with an editor and publisher who value and love the written word and want to spend the time needed in the editorial product so that its opportunities and commercial success are maximized. Small presses, of course, do not have the luxury of publishing financial failures, further stressing the need for all aspects of a book to appear as perfect as possible.

There are imprints in larger publishing houses where line-by-line manuscript editing is still treated as imperative for literary integrity. As mentioned previously, Knopf, a division of Random House, and Algonquin, a division of Workman, are excellent examples. I remember several stories from Larry Brown about how carefully Ms. Ravenel, a co-founder of Algonquin and the editor who discovered the fireman-turned-author, analyzed his works—almost to the point of his annoyance. He wrote with

oOo

— oOo —

a distinct, hard-luck Southern style that created images for the reader of how uneducated, rural whites often lived. Cigarettes were prominent in his scenes, so much so that Mr. Brown disapproved when Ms. Ravenel made a suggestion.

"Larry, there are too many cigarettes in this book," she reportedly told him. "People can't possibly smoke that much."

His reply: "Wanna bet?"

Although he liked to tell stories about her nit-picking of his prose, he had the utmost respect for her and Algonquin, where he wrote for years before moving just before his death to Free Press, a division of Simon and Schuster. A practitioner of *writing quality first, marketing second,* Ms. Ravenel discovered Mr. Brown through an essay he had written in a somewhat obscure literary publication.

"You have any more of these?" she was said to have asked.

By that time, Mr. Brown had been writing for some years during his off time as a fireman for the city of Oxford, Mississippi. He had completed and burned entire novels and maintained a stash of short stories that could have made William Faulkner blush. Ms. Ravenel discovered this quiet and compassionate yet hard-driven writer, helping him develop a core readership following of 25,000 or more, who clung tightly to any word-morsels he would give them. Throughout his success, she reportedly never let up from her stance of tight editing, presuming, I suppose, that her role as a leader in literary publishing was one to be cherished. As a result, it gave Mr. Brown some good fodder with fellow writers at cocktail parties, but the tangible result was timeless works that will be read for years into the future.

— oOo —

—————————— oOo ——————————

Develop Writing Discipline Habits

For most authors, the key to keeping their editor happy is delivering required material on time, according to contract terms. The idea that we have a license to ignore deadlines, turning a finished book into the editor whenever we please, is completely off base in today's profit-first world. My experience has been just the opposite, in fact, considering that when a publisher pays the first half of a significant advance at signing, they want the book to be earning income as quickly as possible.

Therefore, for an author to succeed in the business of writing, they must learn discipline so that when chapters or sections or a finished manuscript are due, calls and e-mails soliciting the material will not have to be made. On my first project, I made getting the book done on deadline a top priority, so I would not earn a reputation out of the gate for being late. Stephen King may be able to turn his work in late because, what can an editor do? David Magee is different, however, and so are you unless you are one of the top percent of the most successful writers in the world, and even many of them have admitted to the pressures of deadline.

My solution is to treat writing pages as exactly what it is—a must-do item for my job. For example, if I have moved past research and conception and into the writing phase of a project, I make notes on my personal "to do" list of what must be accomplished by when. Then, I wake up each morning and try to reach my daily goal before doing anything else. This can be easier said than done, however, and even though I have developed much discipline in several years as a full-time writer, some days get away from me without having tasks completed. And,

—————————— oOo ——————————

oOo

just like an employee on the job, this causes stress and fears that I am falling behind. The simple fact, though, is that a book cannot be completed unless a writer sits down and puts words on paper in a disciplined schedule.

For me, this means a 1,000-words-a-day minimum when I am on deadline for project completion. In terms of page translation this may not sound like much considering it is only three-and-a-half pages of double-spaced text. In the scheme of daily production, it is probably not, either, considering that when I am into the story, have information at hand, and am well rested, I can sit with my laptop in hand and rap out 15 pages or more in one day before my head aches so badly I have to stop. The idea, though, is that on a 1,000-word-per-day schedule, nothing unreasonable has been aspired to and a disciplined routine will yield a book in two to three months with little or no sweat factor. With less stress, the writing is generally better and the profession is more enjoyable.

Some people, like Stephen King, choose to write more words and pages each day. For them, this apparently works well, but probably only because they have been at their job for so long that creating 10 pages per day—or 3,000 words—comes more easily. My theory at this stage of my writing career is to maintain a steady, but non-imposing schedule so that I am never overwhelmed by the tasks. The primary reason being that having to write a book can be one of the most intimidating chores a human can have. I have encountered literally dozens of people who have told me they are beginning work on a manuscript only to see them bogged down in frustration months and years later. It is not that they do not have the ability to write a book.

oOo

——————————————— oOo ———————————————

Instead, in most instances at least, nobody knows if they can do it or not. Intimidated by having to complete the entire project, they focused so much on the enormity of the project that they never got started on the little tasks—daily writing—that ultimately create the book.

How I overcome this is by focusing on the somewhat tired, but effective phrase—*pennies in a jar*—which inspires a person to amass something large by making small, albeit regular contributions. Without thinking that my book must be 250 pages long, I focus only on 1,000 words—or three-and-a-half pages—per day, effectively piling up my "pennies in a jar" so that in two to three months, I have a completed manuscript. To date, this approach has worked and I have only missed deadline by any significant amount for one book, and that was unavoidable considering research was delayed. Therefore, my editors have been pleased for the most part because they did not have to change publication dates, make excuses to publishers and make demanding phone calls to me.

——————————————— oOo ———————————————

Chapter 6

Marketing Matters Most

Despite the editorial nobility of some and the best intentions of many, the reality is that publishing is a business. If there is any lesson in this book worth clinging to, this is it, simple as it may be. Writers searching for the first contract tend to live in a self-absorbed world and often forget this basic fact of enterprise. They are usually so immersed in personal convictions of why their manuscript is worth publishing that they have difficulty stepping back and asking the most basic question: Can this book make money in the marketplace if it is published?

To be certain, that is exactly the question editors and publishers will ask if and when they consider your manuscript. No matter the fluidity of writing or the pragmatism of the prose, if a proposal does not look, feel and smell like money, its chances of finding life in this tough, old world of publishing are slim. You only have to consider the fact that HarperCollins is owned by News Corp., a publicly traded company that must satisfy investors large and small with quarterly and annual earnings. Random House, too, exists as a division of Bertelsmann AG, a global media conglomerate that faces the same demands for rising profits. And Wiley is a publicly traded company, even though family members are still involved in management. Even small Jefferson Press has individual investors anticipating a return on capital. The list can go on because, except for a handful of non-profit publishers, the vast majority must make money. And the only way profitability occurs is if published books deliver revenue in excess of costs. Therefore, when ranking the factors most important to a successful quest to be published, the one at the top must naturally be marketing—tools that move product.

So vital is this function to a book's success that agents, editors and publishers often use it as an excuse for turning down projects that appear to have editorial strengths. The line, "We like it, but we can't figure out how to market it," has been issued so many times that it has become marked as an external joke of the industry. It is the sad song of the failed writer, the excuse used at family gatherings and cocktail parties.

"You haven't been able to find a publisher?"

"No. They liked it but don't know how to sell it."

And, in most cases, that is the honest truth. As much as executives, managers and editors at publishing companies want to believe they are experts at knowing what works and what does not, in terms of selling product to consumers, they actually have very little assurance outside a few standard strategies employed time and time again. When books come along that do not fit into this marketing mold, it is easier to cast them off as opposed to try and figure out ways to make them work.

Develop a Multi-Faceted Plan

What specifically are publishers looking for in regards to book marketability? The simple answer is: anything that works to get books into the hands of readers. There are several very specific points, however, which they believe influence and encourage this to happen, and these are details any writer hoping to land a legitimate publishing contract must work to nail down. For the most part, these marketing items can and should be conveyed in the proposal since it ultimately sells a project to an editor. While the proposal demonstrates to publishers that an author can write, it also indicates whether or not a book has a chance at selling. During editorial acquisition meetings, the proposals for potential books are passed around and analyzed. If someone was able to obtain an outsider-looking-in perspective of these meetings, they would likely see sales and marketing department representatives flipping directly to the section dealing with promotion.

Though before we get fixated on the nuts-and-bolts techniques that work, it is important to cover a primary component of marketability that publishers are increasingly looking for—author marketability. A book is a rather black-and-white item, and for most years it has existed, what the author looked like and how the author presented him or herself did not matter. In today's frenzied media world, that has changed drastically.

———————— oOo ————————

A person who spends any time at all watching major television news networks like CNN or CNBC will quickly realize this, watching reporters from *The Wall Street Journal* and *The New York Times* participating in broadcast interviews. We have reached a point in media where it is no longer enough to report the news, but journalists, and authors too, must visually participate in the news to make more of an impact on audiences, thereby stressing their information and answers.

So, if a prospective author is a talented speaker with dashing looks, a publisher will assume they can actively promote books through addressing pertinent issues with the public and media. An excellent example of this is journalist-turned-author Sebastian Junger, who wrote a popular bestseller titled *A Perfect Storm*. The book was a well-researched, well-written story that likely would have succeeded if Mr. Junger were an ogre. However, the publishing house had in its hands an author who was well-spoken and possessed as well a hip-ish appearance of rugged dash. The broadcast media warmed easily to Mr. Junger, exposing his book to hundreds of thousands of more potential buyers. The result was that not only was his book a bestseller, his ability to self-promote helped make it a blockbuster bestseller.

Publishers have been experiencing similar results in fiction. Take Mr. Grisham as the best example. Considering him to be a handsome man, his publisher, Doubleday, used the entire back cover of one of his first books to expose the author's two-day beard growth appearance. This was a look Mr. Grisham used frequently in public in the early and mid-1990s, developing a persona that held up well on Today Show appearances, which helped build a tremendous fan base among middle-aged

———————— oOo ————————

—————————————— oOo ——————————————

woman, who bought his books by the thousands. This is not to argue falsely that to be a successful author, attractive looks are required. Horror writer Stephen King is not exactly a model candidate with his ultra-thick glasses and bed-head style, though it certainly can be argued that his look fits well with his genre.

For the most part, it depends on what the author is writing as to what type of persona may be suitable, and it is the writer's responsibility to analyze this, crafting a sort of self-brand that can be revealed to the publisher. The author of *Seabiscuit*, Laura Hillenbrand, provides an author mold considerably different from that of Sebastian Junger and John Grisham as she is afflicted with a disease causing extreme fatigue. She is a beautiful woman, as illustrated on the original book jacket, but traveling to Chicago for an hour on Oprah, for instance, would be grueling. What she and the publisher were able to accomplish, though, was incorporating this restricting syndrome into her book promotion story. I have heard her talk in interviews about her difficulty in writing the manuscript and about the extraordinary length of time it took her to complete it. She also has a beautiful voice and does an excellent radio interview, and she wisely focused on this medium as a means to spread the word of her book since she could do it from her home during waking hours. So, by no means is it imperative to have Matt Lauer or Oprah Winfrey charisma or appeal to become a successful author, but it does help when a want-to-be writer completely understands their promotion ability and conveys this to an agent or editor to show how book sales may be helped.

The most compelling author to a publisher, of course, is one who already has a following, either through an established

—————————————— oOo ——————————————

—————————— oOo ——————————

beat on the speaking circuit or through a web site, a newspaper column or any medium that draws a crowd and can be pushed as "low-hanging fruit" for book sales. One book just acquired by Jefferson Press lends itself as an example. The writer is a first-time author whose manuscript is compelling, but there were several reasons for which we could have rejected her proposal. A huge strength, however, was that she maintains a well-designed website that draws more than 20,000 women per month. We figured if some tweaks and minor improvements are made to the site, along with the addition of an active and ongoing blog, this number of hits will rise considerably. With that many women already established as first-tier candidates to buy her book, publishing it made much sense.

The moral of that story is that hopeful writers should consider launching a personal website *before* landing a contract as opposed to after. This commitment may seem premature, and perhaps in reality it is, but when writers need every advantage possible, it turns out to be a step worth taking. For a fiction writer, it could be just the boost needed to separate from the masses and tie down a contract. Take, for example, a writer who has been rejected by almost every agent or editor in the business but knows beyond a doubt that his or her work is worthy of getting into print. Self-publishing or obtaining a vanity publisher will all but ruin their career, but something needs to be done, or they will fall the way of being just another has-been who tried. If this writer were to launch a website, updating it with fresh short stories on a regular basis, and consider writing a blog about their trials of trying to get published, they would have a much improved chance of building an audience over time.

—————————— oOo ——————————

———————————— oOo ————————————

Once webpage hits reach a respectable number, say 20,000 a month, this information should be documented and attached to the marketing page of the proposal, substantiating proof that they have an audience. As a result, this writer's odds of getting a contract just went up significantly.

Perhaps more beneficial to a writer than a successful website is having at their disposal a large number of e-mail addresses, though the two certainly go hand-in-hand. Nobody in the business wants to associate with offensive spam advertisements, and no proof supports their effectiveness in the book industry. But if a writer owns or can obtain opt-in e-mail addresses—meaning e-mail addresses of people who desire to receive notices or offerings—of several hundred thousand or more, publishers will pay attention. Mass e-mailings, when sent to qualified lists and packaged with incentives, are selling books today in large quantities, particularly in non-fiction categories like business and self-help.

Want proof? One writer I am familiar with had a book released by a major publisher in 2005 that was totally ignored by the national chains. For whatever reason, buyers for these companies either did not like the material or did not believe the author had enough credibility to pull it off in the marketplace. Faced with the ultimate challenge of how to sell books when none were available in stores, the author developed a guerilla marketing campaign, attracting buyers to his book at www.amazon.com through a mass e-mail blast to something like six million people. He had purchased the e-mail names for a one-time use from a brokerage company and prepared a crafty pitch to send, telling how he wanted to see his book hit number one on Amazon, and if they would buy today and e-mail their

———————————— oOo ————————————

receipt to a certain address, they could choose between dozens of free gifts of electronic books and articles.

The book did, in fact, reach number one on the Amazon list for a few days, and sales were so significant that I was told the book went back to press two times. The chains never stocked it in any measurable quantity, yet the title sold more than 10,000 units, a credible amount for a no-name writer peddling a how-to book. The publisher could have printed blank pages, and I doubt it would have mattered. The strength of this promotional strategy was its direct approach to buyers, offering items of value in return for their purchase. Some publishers recognize the power of this more than others, but I am quite sure that all will respond positively to the marketing section of proposals, which make note of e-mail lists the author has or can access in order to solicit sales at the time of book publication.

They are not just no-name authors using this e-mail sales tactic, either. To the contrary, some of the biggest names in the business already send e-mails to their contact files and line up advance sales to help propel books to the bestseller list. While I was writing this book, for example, I got not one, but two e-mails from Po Bronson urging me to click on a link to pre-order a signed copy of his upcoming book, *Why Do I Love These People?*, from Powell's, an independent bookstore in Portland, Oregon. Bronson's previous book had been a bestseller, but he was not sitting back on his heels, assuming this one would make it too. According to a note posted on his web site, www.pobron son.com, his e-mail blasts, which did not contain a "buy a book, get other stuff free" gimmick, resulted in more than 2,600 books sold, a figure that apparently amused even a successful writer

———————— oOo ————————

like himself. Make no mistake, the publisher was amused also. Even a large company like Random House, moving millions of units, has reason to get excited about one author selling 2,600 units through one independent store. If Bronson had merely showed up at Powell's for a launch event signing, there is no amount of promotion that could have brought in 2,600 buyers; one hundred, maybe, but definitely not 2,600.

Another marketing advantage publishers like to see is an author who spends a lot of time on the road, speaking to audiences about their subject of expertise. In non-fiction, this remains one of the vital tricks-of-the-trade when it comes to getting books sold. The long-running business bestseller *Good to Great* by Jim Collins may be the best model for this that I know. A genuine bestseller on its own merits through retail sales, this book has experienced an unprecedented run as a hardback original because Collins speaks at corporations and on university campuses all over the world. He collects a nice fee for his time, but the real payoff comes from his ability to tie book sales in with his appearances. If, for instance, he addresses 750 quality managers at General Motors, each of the attendees will be given a book. This practice has kept *Good to Great* among this country's leading bestselling titles since its release in October, 2001. As a result, Collins can command higher fees, and as arguably the bestselling business author ever in the world, he will be poised to garner on his next book an advance north of $10 million.

In addition to speaking, authors need to try and link to national and regional associations whenever possible, pointing this out clearly in proposals. For example, I write a newspaper column

———————— oOo ————————

—————————— oOo ——————————

on the side for a daily paper and belong to a national association of columnists. If I were to write a book about working as a columnist or journalist, I would be wise to seek the endorsement of this columnist association before my proposal was completed and insert it prominently in the marketing section.

One tactic many hopeful authors try, which carries little weight with large publishers, is writing into the proposal that they will spend up to a certain amount of their own money to market a title. Small publishers appreciate this since they are always looking for cost-sharing plans. Bigger publishers, though, can fund advertising budgets however they see fit, and such an offering to them signals that an author might get into their business unnecessarily. They would rather see authors willing to chip in on marketing costs under specific areas detailed in the proposal, like offering to purchase up to five million qualified e-mail addresses to use as the backbone of a direct campaign.

Another reason why the commitment to spend a certain amount of dollars carries little weight is the fact that advertising really does not sell books. When publishers buy space, it is to support an already successful book or author or to help spread a specific agenda. They have learned, painfully, that the book-buying public is too discerning to fall into an ad trap. Therefore, the publishing strategy relies primarily on public relations efforts to launch books—focusing on key appearances, media interviews, reviews, notices in the form of e-mails and newsletters to interested groups and associations, and word-of-mouth. If a book gains unusually good reviews or proves through its initial attention that it will breakout, ad dollars are usually allocated according to anticipated sales and print run. It is rarely

—————————— oOo ——————————

a front-end decision, meaning that an author's promise to spend
$10,000 promotional dollars, not earmarked, does not compare
to a detailed plan, targeting specific people.

Equating Sales with Success

Once a hopeful writer gets an idea of how he or she can best
position their marketing talents and resources to facilitate a
manuscript sale, they will be well served to spend time researching and trying to understand the general levels of sales that are
taking place in the industry. Most people, without a doubt,
have a distorted idea of how many books authors generally sell.
James Patterson may sell more than a million units each time
he has a new title released, but David Magee does not, nor does
Tom Franklin nor Po Bronson nor Michael Lewis. In fact, to
make a qualified bestseller list, like those published by *The Wall
Street Journal* or *The New York Times*, all a book has to sell in
some circumstances is 10,000 or more. That's hard to imagine,
I know, but I have a couple of very specific case studies to support this claim. For starters, common knowledge in publishing
holds that 7,500 units per week, if moved through the proper
counted channels, will deliver an appearance on a bestseller list.
One writer I am familiar with proved this, the hard way.

Desperately wanting to make a major list to raise his speaking
appearance fees, the author of one non-fiction book arranged
with two retailers of a national chain to purchase in person
8,000 units in one week. Half were bought in one region of the
country, and the other half were bought in another region. The
author told managers of the stores that if the sale did not appear
on Nielson's Bookscan, an industry source for tracking books

sold at the retail level, he would return them all the next week. Needless to say, the units did appear in Bookscan, and the title debuted at number one on the *Wall Street Journal* non-fiction list despite selling less than 250 units to traditional buyers in the same week. Today, the author can boast that he is bestselling, even though it came at a price—more than $125,000 and knowledge that he defrauded the system. The point, however, is not about how to get on a list the hard way, but that the numbers driving bestsellers are smaller than many people think.

It sometimes happens that large publishers like Harper-Collins and Random House will release a book that gets no attention from the trade or media and ultimately sells fewer than 5,000 copies. I can recall one book in recent years that has not yet sold more than 1,000 units according to Bookscan, despite the fact that the author got publicity on CNN and other national news programs.

What then constitutes a success? That, of course, depends on the publisher and how much cost is in the book. Remember, publishing is a business. If a book is profitable and has redeeming value in the public domain, then I rule it a success. Publishers will often have an author believe that a book has not performed unless the author totally recoups his or her advance, but this is more often used as a tactic to negotiate a lower advance the next time around if the book returns a profit. The truth is, if a book is in the black, the editor and the publisher are quite happy.

At Jefferson Press, profitability can occur when a book sells 5,000 units or more. We often acquire books that have break-even points of several thousand units in raw dollars, meaning that once they sell above this mark, they can cover pro-rata share of overhead and general operating expenses. At Simon and Schuster, an editor would probably be less than thrilled with any book selling under 10,000 units since they are more concerned with homerun opportunities in the business. One thing hopeful authors should know, however, is that selling 5,000 or 10,000 units is much more difficult than it sounds. I know of one extremely talented fiction writer who received a starred review from *Publisher's Weekly*, a raving review from *The New York Times*, and had multiple big-name authors dubbing him a star on the rise, yet his book sold less than 8,000 units. Another writer and acquaintance of mine was "sure" he could manufacture from his marketing genius 15,000 units sold. "If I can't do that," he once said, "something is wrong." Last time I checked, he had sold 800 units.

On my first book, I was very fortunate to have translation rights sold in seven languages, resulting in global exposure for a very international story. *Turnaround* was a top-seller among business books in France, as it was in Japan and in Brazil. It also sold well in China and in the United States, totaling to date more than 100,000 units sold. For any writer, outside of Stephen King and John Grisham types, this is a success. Subsequent titles of mine have sold anywhere from 18,000 units to date with four translations still to be published to 28,000 units to date with three translations still to be published. Profitably speaking, these books are successes, and considering they are in the business category at a time when demand in that area has floundered for several years, I am quite pleased.

Having an understanding of such numbers is critical to being

oOo

able to enter the realm of publishing because agents and editors loathe the unrealistic dreamer, who is sure he or she holds the next *Seabiscuit*, poised to sell hundreds of thousands of copies no matter what. That is not to say your book or anyone else's does not have the potential of selling a million copies. I am utterly convinced that in the next five years I will have a block-buster bestseller, and I expect this to occur sooner rather than later. But when I approach my agent or editors about projects and how I can help support the book through marketing, I deal with base realities, helping them to better understand how I can ensure project profitability. In the end, all they want is for the author to show with specifics how they can help a book meet its bottom-line expectations.

oOo

Chapter 7

Your Writing Must Be Good

I am absolutely convinced that marketing matters most, but there is more to getting published than having strong sales components. Just because publishers need a clear idea that a book can generate sales before they issue a contract, this does not mean that reputable ones will publish anything simply for the sake of profit. There remains the issue of editorial strength and integrity. Quality of writing still matters — a lot.

This is one reason agents and editors do not like telephone calls from people with whom they do not already have a formal relationship. The publishing industry is based on the written word after all, and if you want to participate, you must prove that you can clearly communicate your thoughts and ideas through query letters and proposals. Industry professionals can

———————————— oOo ————————————

detect the novice almost every time because of their tendency to want to talk on the telephone, vocally explaining all of the reasons that make their project worthy.

"If you'll just give me a minute," the novice will say, "I think you will know why this idea is so good, and you've got to have it."

The general rule of thumb in the industry is to quickly get off of the phone, since listening to a spoken pitch from a non-professional usually results in a waste of time. The best example of this I can give comes from a writer who contacted me in 2005 about publishing a title of his through Jefferson Press. Like others on the publishing side of the business, the one thing I never, ever want to do is discuss a title with a prospective writer about which I have seen nothing on paper. I do not want them to verbalize their book; I want them to *show* me they can write it.

One afternoon, however, an unpublished writer with a project of seeming promise persuaded me to do the dreaded — make a phone call to talk in advance of reading a single word. He had heard about Jefferson Press through an industry contact and made a phone call to one of our business partners, pushing the merits of his project. A message was passed along to me to call the man at my convenience, and the quick overview from my partner grabbed my interest, admittedly.

The man claimed to have written a book that described the oddest named towns and cities in America and explained how they received their names. Places such as Intercourse, Pennsylvania and Alligator, Mississippi would come to life in a book serving both historians and seekers of Americana. Recognizing the marketability of the project and its quirky "Today Show"

———————————— oOo ————————————

———————————————— oOo ————————————————

type of appeal, I kept a small slip of paper with the man's name and number on top of my desk, planning to make the call when time presented itself.

Before one full day passed, however, I received an e-mail from my business partner that the gentleman had called him again, this time expressing eagerness to talk to someone with editorial responsibilities. Irritated, I shot back a reply to my partner, aimed at his caller.

"Well," I wrote, "he may have a decent project, but he just failed rule number one of Publishing 101. He does not understand this business demands patience and no phone calls."

My enthusiasm for the project abated, greatly. A man making over-eager telephone calls could not possibly hold in his possession a book worth spending thousands of dollars to acquire, publish and market. I did not want him to continue calling my partner, however, so I grabbed a telephone and dialed the man's number. When he did not answer, I was thrilled with the prospects of avoiding dialogue altogether. A message, I thought, would suffice. In his voice inbox, I left clear instructions about how to proceed.

"Thanks for your call," I said. "In this business, there is not much to talk about, though, in the early stages. What I need you to do is mail a few sample chapters and a table of contents or some kind of outline to me. I'll take a look at it and get back to you in a week or two."

Two hours later, my telephone rang. Having gleaned my number from his caller identification, the writer dialed my number, not satisfied with the voice mail I left. Mailing a sample of his writing was not good enough either. Like most unpublished

———————————————— oOo ————————————————

writers, he wanted to talk about his project. Realizing he was not going away, I began to listen to what he had to say. Personable and easy with conversation, he launched from the first minute into all the reasons why his book was publishable and how it would make a lot of money.

Admittedly, I was lured into his verbalized account. His working title was not only good, it was outstanding. The concept sounded completely marketable, and he had a son working for a global news organization. Perhaps the man had a publishable manuscript after all. How he slipped through the cracks of an agent or every other editor he had tried to call before reaching us, I did not know. He had me believing, though, that it was worthy and ready to roll directly onto bookshelves around the country.

"This sounds great," I told him.

But then I remembered I was shattering rule number one. I had never seen a word the man had written. As good as his project sounded, experience told me that his writing might not be of the quality that he espoused. Common sense took control again, easing my excitement.

"We might as well quit talking," I said. "What I need to do is see your work. Mail it to our post office box, and I'll take a look. Otherwise, there's nothing more to talk about until I have seen it."

As luck would have it, the man lived in the area. Instead of mailing the manuscript, he would simply have it dropped off the very next morning. No sense wasting valuable time. Waiting on me in the office upon arrival at 10 a.m. the next day was a complete manuscript, bound together in a three-ring notebook.

———————————————— oOo ————————————————

Without delay, I took a look, examining two essays on different small towns that were facing each other in the open-page
notebook. Within 15 seconds, I knew—the writing was not as
strong as I had hoped.

His writer's research was good, his concept was excellent, the
working title was can't-miss, but the writing missed the mark.
Leads were all too similar, dealing with nuts-and-bolts facts like
location and population, and there was no crafty narrative to
draw readers in to what could potentially be compelling, historic
stories about how oddly dubbed cities and towns were named.
I shut the notebook and within three minutes had e-mailed the
writer, delivering the bad news.

"I'm sorry," I wrote.

You can probably guess the man's response. Not satisfied with
my e-mail, he picked up his telephone and called me, again.
This time, I did not answer, hoping he would resort to e-mail.
Within minutes, my inbox did in fact blacken, showing I had
one new message. In it, the man thanked me for taking the time
to consider his book, but he also asked me to take the time to
give specific instances of how he could improve his work.

Almost no editor or agent I know would take the time to tell
a want-to-be-writer how to change their work for anything less
than serious compensation. As a full-time non-fiction writer, I
get paid for my editorial abilities, whatever they may be. There
is certainly nothing that I enjoy more than helping someone
succeed in this business, but that does not mean I have the time
or interest to dole out editorial advice. If he could not write the
book himself, then perhaps he is not cut out to be an author.

The man's actions were understandable. He was eager to

———————————————— oOo ————————————————

—————————————— oOo ——————————————

get published and willing to ask for any favor that might help achieve that goal. If he had taken the time to consider the reality and extent of this work, that asking me to make major editorial suggestions is no different than calling up his lawyer and asking that legal briefs be drawn up and filed for free in his behalf, he likely would not have inquired. Still, I rejected the request.

"You've got to figure out how to write these stories on your own," I replied. "I can't do it for you."

Interesting enough, I liked the man, but I still dealt with him quickly and in a straightforward manner, trying to let him know the truth before he wasted an unreasonable amount of time trying to get a book into print that was not ready. Longer term, the book might succeed, especially if he finds a co-writer or learns to better present the work himself. As it was, however, the book had no chance because, despite a catchy title and an outstanding market outline, the writing simply did not meet the standards that publishers demand.

Substance and Style

As a general rule, editors are an intelligent lot, and as such, they like to be associated with quality literary works. While focusing on the bottom line may keep them employed, pride sharpens their desire of bringing to life works of real merit. The same can be said for many agents, who initially entered the publishing industry because they are romanticized by great books and enjoy bringing great, new manuscripts to print.

So we can joke about a book being able to succeed with a great marketing plan "even if it had blank pages," but the truth

—————————————— oOo ——————————————

oOo

is that most editors and agents hold themselves to a higher standard, regardless of the primary emphasis placed on marketing. Marketing may help a work of adequate writing make the cut, but poor writing rarely gets through the cracks in the competitive world of high-end publishing. The reason being that, with what seems like one out of every two people in America writing a book, getting an agent or editor to take a look at pages with poorly structured storylines and weak prose is almost impossible—there are too many other choices available.

Most agents and editors see so many submissions on a regular basis that they can spot loose and sloppy writing and the careless style of novices within seconds of looking at a manuscript. Then they will quickly hurl it toward the trash can, marketing plan be damned. It is true, though, that experienced writers can pull off getting into print works of less-than-desirable quality, and some do this frequently, often with considerably strong sales. Hopeful writers, however, cannot expect to get a foot in the door without showing an ability to spin a good and interesting story.

The problem, of course, is that most people do not know what qualifies as good writing, and they allow themselves to make continual submissions that have no chance of acceptance. Take the persistent man mentioned above, for example. He had the credentials of a good education and even spent many years as a school teacher and administrator himself. He has read more than his share of works and speaks with a knowledgeable flair, but for whatever reason, he did not recognize what distinguishes good writing from bad. It is not that he had to write scholarly essays or complicated prose like William Faulkner to get a contract, but even in regard to nuts-and-bolts non-fiction and less

oOo

oOo

academic ventures, a certain line of quality must be crossed for a work to be acquisition-worthy.

A prime example is my first book. Although I had been named one of the leading newspaper columnists in Mississippi when I was in my early 20's and was known for an ability to turn a phrase, I was relatively inexperienced in the craft of book writing when I got my first contract. As a result, my first project came off at times like a series of long newspaper feature articles. Some reviewers, like one from the *Boston Globe*, said as much, in fact. The book still sold well, becoming an international business hit, because I had a strong subject and because I at least had the sense not to try and compensate for my inexperience by overwriting it.

The book supports the concept that decent writing can suffice when the story is big enough to stand on its own. Certainly, there are sections in the book where the writing finds higher ground, but overall, I see some large, unfilled holes when I look back on it today. If I were to rewrite the book now, there is no question it would be stronger editorially. But honestly, I doubt it would have sold any more copies since what I produced worked fine, containing enough structure and core elements of good writing to earn some very nice reviews. Several major publications, like *The Harvard Business Review*, said it was a must-read case study, and, most importantly, it was good enough to launch a writing career.

Besides, my acquiring editor knew when considering my proposal that I was a first-time author and minor problems would inevitably result. But from the proposal, he could see that I understood the basics, including the value of having

oOo

strong chapter leads, the importance of layering information, the need for tight writing, and the benefits of keeping the reader moving along. Above all, he saw that I understood that when writing a business book, lessons learned must be made very clear to the reader.

The problem is that most want-to-be writers are not submitting work even close to a satisfactory level. They may be able to pick up a book like my first and knock holes in it in every direction, but when it comes to producing sentences, paragraphs and pages on their own, their work will resemble something more characteristic of an eighth grader than that of a publishable author.

Consider one manuscript that was submitted to Jefferson Press last year by a self-professed psychopath. A schizophrenic with bipolar disorder, the man had what seemed in query form to be a good and worthy project, explaining how trauma from 9/11 led him into a mental downfall, ending his professional career and happiness. I could tell the writing was less-than-desirable after two minutes but continued a few pages into the manuscript out of curiosity of the story. By around the third page, however, an odd line grabbed my attention. Writing about his former girlfriend, the man referred to her as a "fuckturd."

Inserting such a vulgar, nonsense word into text with no obvious reason was poor choice enough, but the man made it far worse by interrupting his already disjointed tale to explain in complete detail what in the world a "fuckturd" is, rambling into a description that, as I recall, said it is the "little piece of poo that gets stuck to the hair on a dog's butt." When I told this man through an e-mail follow-up that we had no interest in

_____ oOo _____

publishing his book, he e-mailed back within minutes, stating that he was in a hospital, near death. Would I consider changing my mind? When told no again, he fired back a bit of a belligerent response, and I thought I might have to call him a certain eight-letter name. Soon enough, however, he left me alone, no doubt launching into an inquisition with another unsuspecting publisher.

The question that begs to be asked from this is, what quality of writing does a novice have to deliver to get a publishing contract? The answer is different, according to the specific genre. In commercial fiction, the only way a non-published author can typically break through is with exceptional writing that is paralleled by few in the field. There are dozens upon dozens of agents in New York at this minute holding in their possession fiction manuscripts of the highest literary quality they have unsuccessfully shopped to editors at publishing houses of all sizes. The problem is that most of these houses are acquiring not more than a handful of new fiction authors to launch each year, and if hopeful writers cannot set themselves apart with writing quality, the chances are slim that they will rise to the top of the slush pile.

So difficult is it to launch new fiction authors that a recent story I read in a major newspaper cited editors who said it simply costs too much to launch new fiction writers when the big, proven ones like John Grisham corner the market. It is much more cost-effective for publishers to invest in non-fiction, books with clear and defined subjects, because if marketed properly, these can at least achieve respectable sales that recover investment. With commercial fiction, a small handful of authors are

_____ oOo _____

———————————— oOo ————————————

earning the larger portion of all industry sales while dozens of others barely make a showing when combined together. The simple fact, then, is that with fewer publishers willing to invest in new fiction writers, their quality of writing must be nothing less than exceptional.

Before you jump to conclusions and suggest that your work is better than or at least as good Mr. Grisham's since his style is mostly straightforward, plot-based work, let me say that you may be missing something. Quality writing does not always refer to an author's ability to deliver poetry. Commercial fiction, which Mr. Grisham writes, is not produced easily or carelessly. The masses of readers have styles and formulas they like, and only certain writers know how to tap into this. For this reason Grisham can sell two million units of a title while talented writers I know, who may be labeled creative but admit to yearning for mass sales, cannot obtain many more than 25,000 units sold. And while it is true that the writing of leading commercial authors may be straightforward, they must nevertheless craft excellent plots, tight storylines, and strong characters. Simply put, it is harder to please two million people than it is to creatively write a book that amuses a few thousand.

The preference of publishers makes this genre even tougher to break into as they would much rather stick with their proven commodities, even if their work slips a bit here and there, because they have the shelf-space command and reader trust, and very little professional risk, if any at all, is involved. At the top, there is only room for a few, making it next to impossible for a hopeful to break into the world of commercial fiction. In fact, I have often told people that they have a better chance of making

———————————— oOo ————————————

—————————————————— oOo ——————————————————

the roster of an NBA team than they do of becoming the next John Grisham.

Oddly, it may be easier for a writer to develop a career in the area of literary fiction than commercial fiction since writing with a creative emphasis offers more leeway for rougher edges. When perusing such work, editors and readers tend to grant more literary license, with the work's quality often resting in the eye of the beholder. What one reader or editor sees as babble, another sees as colorfully indicative of a time, a place or a passion. Larry Brown had a knack for bringing rural roughnecks to life, but he did so in a manner that could be considered crude by some purists. Larry was successful, though, because he wrote from experience and from his heart and was not afraid to weave character-driven tales, scented with colloquial and human awkwardness. At times, his writing could require some work by the reader, but fans of Southern literature loved his books, and him, with few questioning his talent.

Writing a tight, commercial package that was largely plot-driven was not Mr. Brown's forte, though his storylines were certainly complex. He was, however, a creative writer who specialized in painting vivid details of people and place, taking the reader into a world of cigarettes and plain truths with unique ability. He worked harder than any writer I have ever known to develop his skill, and he was not afraid to burn an entire completed manuscript because he believed it was not good enough.

Because they both lived in Oxford, Mississippi at the same time their writing careers were emerging, Mr. Brown and Mr. Grisham were friends and had strong mutual respect for the work of each other. Both, however, had full recognition and respect of

—————————————————— oOo ——————————————————

———————————— oOo ————————————

their differences. Mr. Grisham delivered the commercial package, selling millions of books around the world. Mr. Brown delivered the creative landscape, and while the advances and royalties he earned were far superior to the minuscule pay he had received as a fireman, they were mere pennies compared to the earnings of Mr. Grisham. In a good year, Larry Brown sold 25,000 books, if that. In a so-so year, Mr. Grisham sells 2,500,000 books.

Mr. Brown had a solid and feverishly supportive fan base, but it was one that was limited by the Southern literary nature of his writing and his hard-knock plots. He was pleased with the trappings, however, because in succeeding as a creative writer, he may have suffered from fewer sales and, therefore, fewer dollars, but he had a wide literary space to work in, able to fling words and concepts around liberally. Those of us fortunate enough to know both during their peak of popularity in the 1990s occasionally laughed that John would trade all of his millions for the freedom to write like Larry. And we were not joking.

But as talented as Mr. Brown was—some consider him the South's most superlative voice of the past 25 years—finding an opening in his genre is easier than in Mr. Grisham's for the simple fact that, with works of literary fiction, more emphasis is put on the voice than on the pureness of writing. If someone tells me they aim to be the next John Grisham, I will roll my eyes, hinting strongly at the impossibility. But if someone tells me they want to be the next Larry Brown, I would say to them, work night and day at the craft, submit your work time and time again despite repeated rejection, and establish a new voice. Then, it very well might happen.

In non-fiction, of course, the quality of writing is not nearly

———————————— oOo ————————————

oOo

as important. It has to be good enough, but it does not have to break or bend established standards of excellence. As mentioned previously, my first book was not exactly a masterpiece of words, yet it has sold thus far more than 100,000 copies and is still going strong. People buy non-fiction books in most cases because they want to take elements from them applicable in their own lives.

Even in narrative non-fiction, readers typically are more interested in gleaning lessons learned than anything else. Therefore, non-fiction does not mandate the highest level of writing, and it is possible for a writer to actually be too sophisticated for this genre. What works best is clear and explicit writing that shows—not tells—the reader the facts and truth of a subject through a well-organized, well-structured sequence of bookworthy depth and cohesiveness.

That does not mean a book will sell 100,000 copies if a writer delivers a well-written project. My second book, *Ford Tough*, was one of the top business book releases in America in October 2004, and it was far superior editorially to my first book. The book did okay sales-wise, but it did not achieve the same level as my first book because the subject did not resonate as well or as true with buyers. It was either a story they already knew or a story they did not care as much about.

Similarly, writing a decently crafted non-fiction book or proposal does not mean that agents and editors will want the work no matter what. Just as there are many manuscripts of merit floating around in fiction circles, there are hundreds of pitches being made on non-fiction books where the writing is of sufficient quality. The dividing line then becomes issues of subject and marketability. But if you have paid your dues

oOo

———————————— oOo ————————————

and learned the craft of writing so that you can deliver pages of text that are at least respectable, you will not have to resort to bothering publishing's powers-that-be on the telephone, trying to verbalize to them how great of a writer you are.

———————————— oOo ————————————

Chapter 8

Why Good Books Often Don't Sell (and Bad Ones Do)

Book publishing is one of the most unusual industries one can find, because product quality often has little to do with one's success or failure in the trade. Unfair as it may be and odd as it may seem, some of the best written works fail as business propositions while books of the most illiterate garble often turn out to make money. Understanding this irony is perhaps one of the most important aspects of learning the business of writing, because many promising careers have been ruined by the crushing blows of reality against expectation.

Like post-partum depression afflicting women after childbirth, coming face-to-face with the fact that a good book is not selling can send a sales-deserving writer into a deep and prolonged sadness. Able to crush years of research, planning and working

— oOo —

toward success within a matter of weeks, it is the ultimate insult and one a writer can barely stand. Having been rejected first by agents and then by editors, the author has been living in bliss ever since that first deal was struck. The biggest stress was completing the manuscript to satisfaction, and once that task is completed and the book arrives hot-off-the-press, the tendency is to want to pop a cork and celebrate the completed journey.

Without a doubt, a party would be well-justified. Crossing the transom and becoming a legitimately published author is no easy task. Whether the work is creative fiction or nuts-and-bolts non-ficton, months—or even years—were spent toiling over words, sentences and pages in an effort to create a book able to stand on its own as well-crafted and conceived. In place of the internal questions roused by multiple rejections, pride swells at the moment of publication, along with burgeoning hopes that bestseller lists and critical acclaim await. The problem, however, is that reaching publication is only part of getting published, and the period immediately following a book's release often proves to be the most difficult aspect of the business of writing and leaves important lessons to be learned.

For months, there have been well-intentioned comments to the author from friends and family like, "You're going to be rich!" and "I'm sure it will be a bestseller." They have read the book, liked it, and have no reason to suspect it will not be well-received, especially since the average person thinks all books they have seen in Barnes and Noble shelves sell thousands and thousands of copies, earning the author handsome royalties. Nine times out of ten, however, the book will not meet the author's sales expectations, and the lukewarm reception

— oOo —

oOo

from the trade, reviewers and, sometimes, even friends will be a disconcerting experience, more troubling than any of the other setbacks along the way.

Readers Don't Always Relate

There are so many examples of baffling, bad sales that I could look just about anywhere and find a book that has performed below expectations. After all, only a tiny fraction of new books actually break through, achieving surprising sales results or legitimate bestseller status. The example I use most frequently in talks to writers' groups is Tom Franklin and his exceptional novel *Hell at the Breech* (William Morrow, 2003), mentioned previously in this book. For Mr. Franklin and his first-ever novel, plans at release had gone according to the publisher's best imagination. Galley copies sent in advance of publication to stir attention did just that, creating a well-qualified industry buzz. Word in the trade publications and on the proverbial publishing street was that the former Grisham Writer-in-Residence at the University of Mississippi had followed up his successful initial work, a collection of short stories (*Poachers*), with a work of Faulkneresque proportion.

"This is historical fiction at its best," stated a starred review of *Hell at the Breech* in the American Library Association newsletter *Booklist*.

For several years, Franklin had worked meticulously on his novel, fine-tuning scenes and descriptions, so it would translate so vividly to readers they would never imagine it to be contemporary fiction based on 1890s fact. But despite the glowing reviews and despite the best efforts of the publisher, the book

oOo

———————————— oOo ————————————

never took off at the retail level. Agonizingly, he had to endure some signings at bookstores around the country where one or two people showed up. It was at times a humiliating experience that only a writer who has gone through the same situation can relate with.

Some independent stores with a particularly knowledgeable reader base did well with the book, but most did not. Adding more insult, the book underperformed in the national chain stores. Here is an epic work of considerable proportion that was well-reviewed and highly thought of by booksellers, but consumers never warmed to it in quantity for whatever reason. *Hell at the Breach* is good, if not great, but it became yet another in a long line of credible works that did not meet expectations. Fortunately for Mr. Franklin, his talent will keep the book alive for years to come, and if he ever experiences one major break-through book, fans will no doubt return to his original novel in large numbers. There are no guarantees, however, and for now a good work remains widely unappreciated.

In publishing, this happens all the time, even in non-fiction, a genre that is much easier to sell at the retail level. An example of this that I frequently use is a book published in November 2003 by HarperBusiness. *Tragic Indifference: One Man's Battle with the Auto Industry Over the Danger of SUVs*, by Adam Penenberg, a title I followed closely at publication because it is about the Ford Explorer-Firestone tire debacle. Since I was writing a book about Ford Motor Company—specifically one about the leadership of Chairman and CEO William Clay (Bill) Ford Jr.—the story with details of the Explorer rollover incidents was intriguing. Published by one of this country's

———————————— oOo ————————————

—— oOo ——

leading business imprints and written by an author with a credible track record, I figured *Tragic Indifference* would be a big industry hit. Released during the peak of the fall season, it was no doubt a major player in the HarperBusiness lineup for 2003, and immediately upon publication, Mr. Penenberg could be seen granting interviews on large media outlets. Personally, I recall once seeing him answer questions about the book on CNN and remember hearing a national radio broadcast that mentioned the book as well.

With access to Tab Turner, the lawyer credited with developing and breaking the Explorer-Firestone rollover case, Mr. Penenberg had a whale of a story to tell, piecing together for readers for the first time exactly how it became a national story and how it unfolded all along the way. Also giving the book apparent credibility were the sold movie rights, calling for Michael Douglas to star in and direct a motion picture based on the book. Seemingly, all of the needed ingredients were in place for a breakout book.

In reality, though, the book failed miserably. Research through Nielson's Bookscan, which tracks retails sales in the trade, some six months after publication, revealed that less than 500 units had been sold. That's not a typo you just saw; the number is correct—less than 500 units sold despite the fact that the book was credible, reasonably well-written and was backed by a leading publishing house. And let's not forget that the author appeared on national cable television to promote the book, and it was reviewed in such national media as *USA Today*, *The San Francisco Chronicle* and *The Boston Globe*.

The problem, best as I could surmise, was that the large

—— oOo ——

oOo

national chains never bought into the book because of its law-suit-played-out-in-words nature, and, therefore, it never got major display promotion. Second, the book was an exposé case involving a car and a tire, which nobody cared much about. The author tried and had some success bringing characters to life like the attorney, Mr. Turner, and a few victims of rollover crashes. Still, the book was about a car and a tire, and even though the case received extensive national media attention, Ford was largely vindicated, and when the book came out, the Explorer was still one of the top-selling vehicles in America. Readers simply did not care, so books stocked by retailers were returned en mass a few months after publication, and *Tragic Indifference* was probably written off by the publisher as a big expense. A skilled journalist, the author is no doubt left having to overcome the industry-spurning scar of having his name on a book that did not exceed even 1,000 units through the trade.

It is likely not his fault, of course. In its purest form, the book was good, but the market was apparently limited. My book about Ford had some sales issues of its own, underperforming according to very high expectations. The story of Bill Ford Jr. is a captivating one, and the book I wrote was good. The publisher and buyers with the national chains, along with myself, believed the book had a bestseller quality. Large quantities were stocked in stores from coast to coast, and we planned to make some serious noise. But because the comeback of Ford Motor Company was not coming together as planned, the story lacked significant reader buy-in, and the book underperformed.

Fortunately, because Bill Ford is an intriguing character and this book was the first to explore his personality and leadership

oOo

— oOo —

style—and because Ford employees warmed to its generally positive nature—the book sold considerably better than *Tragic Indifference*, allowing my career to continue without too much pain and delay.

For me, though, there were *tough* lessons learned. First of all, my eyes were opened first-hand to the fact that good books do not always sell. My work on that past manuscript was solid and the writing of quality, but reviewers panned me or ignored me at every turn, probably because they viewed the book as too positive. The reality was that from the moment at which I started the book, Ford Motor Company was in such dreadful shape that when I concluded the story, the company had clearly made positive strides and what I wrote was simply the truth. I pointed out clearly in *Ford Tough* that major problems still existed at Ford, but it did not seem to matter to readers. The bottom line was that being a good book was not enough to propel it to bestseller status, and it, too, had the fate of returns at the retail level.

People Need a Reason to Buy

Sometimes, however, the complete opposite happens, and books that are marginally well-written, having relatively low publisher and trade expectations, find life and become an industry surprise that stokes a publisher's bottom line. The best example of this I have witnessed is the book *More Than a Pink Cadillac: Mary Kay's Nine Leadership Keys to Success,* written by John Underwood and published by McGraw Hill in 2002. With access to the company, seasoned author Underwood created a lessons primer aimed at pointing out which characteristics primed the success for this independent, sales representative-based cosmetics company.

— oOo —

———————— oOo ————————

The problem was that writing a business book about a makeup company was a stretch. The book was thin and based on such sales force mantra's as "make me feel important!" and "OK never does it; you've got to be great." In fact, the book was so lacking in meaty material that word in the publishing scene was that internal expectations of it were low. Because the company supported the book, however, and had a deep and loyal independent sales force, marketing efforts to the Mary Kay representatives around the world paid off and sales took off, far exceeding expectations.

More Than a Pink Cadillac became a *New York Times* business bestseller, surprising many in the industry, including a handful at McGraw-Hill, who probably suspected they possessed a lacking editorial product that would never succeed outside of internal sales. Fueled by the bestseller status, however, the book was stocked in very high quantities in the national chains, producing a big hit for McGraw-Hill, the author and Mary Kay due to resulting publicity. Trade publications, ironically, had totally ignored the book. *Publisher's Weekly*, for instance, did not review it, nor did any of the major newspapers. But the book was a success by all industry measurements because it far-exceeded revenue expectations and gave McGraw-Hill a bona fide bestseller. The majority of sales may have resulted online from direct mail and e-mail efforts targeted at Mary Kay's sales reps, but that did not matter. The book sold because thousands of company representatives wanted it and was a success, giving strength to the argument that marketing matters most. Good books do not always sell, but books with strong marketing components in place usually do.

———————— oOo ————————

—— oOo ——

Another example of a not-so-great book selling beyond expectations is one published by Wiley in 2005 about Apple CEO Steve Jobs. *iCon Steve Jobs: The Greatest Second Act in the History of Business* by Jeffrey S. Young and William L. Simon, is an outside-perspective biography of one of the hottest corporate leaders in America in this era. Since the authors had no access to Mr. Jobs, this book would presumably have fallen into the so-so success category. But apparently because Mr. Young had written a Jobs biography published in 1987, which the Apple CEO did not like, the company retaliated against publication of *iCon Steve Jobs*, going so far as to contact executives at Wiley and demand the book not be released without changes. News reports suggest Wiley officials did not agree, pushing ahead with publication plans and as a result, Apple removed Wiley titles such as *Mac for Dummies* from all of its retail stores. News of this reached the media, making business headlines all over the world, and a book that had little chance of becoming a bestseller rocketed in online presales and bookstore orders.

None of this, of course, had to do with the book's editorial quality. Sales resulted purely from publicity which delivered hype of an over-sensitive CEO and a literary work that promised to deliver juicy, page-turning details of his life. Though once the book became available for sale and reading consumption, some people questioned it in regard to editorial quality as well as integrity. Complaints were made that the book was not well-organized by the authors and that it simply rehashed too much old information. One reviewer took it much farther, though, claiming plagiarism, one of the nastiest accusations a journalist and author can face.

—— oOo ——

———————————— oOo ————————————

"Every author wants his work to influence later tellings," wrote reviewer Alan Deutschman in the *San Francisco Chronicle*, "but hey, guys, this is kind of pushing it. I don't know whether I should feel flattered or ask for my fair share of the book's royalties."

Mr. Deutschman had written a Jobs biography, *The Second Coming of Steve Jobs*, that was published by Broadway on September 11, 2001. For obvious reasons, the book never got much exposure despite being well-written. Fate in publishing often has its way, for better or for worse, and this *iCon Steve Jobs* is a prime example. The supposed theory of what occurred is that Mr. Young took his first book, which covered the initial success of Steve Jobs, and intertwined it with research from Mr. Deutschman's book, which covered the second act of Mr. Jobs' success. Mr. Deutschman cried foul in his review, ironically creating still more attention for *iCon Steve Jobs*.

Ultimately, there was more negative than positive news printed and spoken about the book, but this helped far more than it hurt in the end, allowing a book with questionable editorial quality to succeed. More than anything, this shows why non-fiction books sell more units as a general rule than fiction. Writing quality is always an issue, but in non-fiction, it is often overcome by other factors, such as unusual publicity and targeted marketing efforts.

As mentioned previously, that is why publishers are far less interested in contracting no-name, first-time authors for books than they are in contracting known personalities capable of generating news headlines, with books about subjects for which the author has natural marketing tie-ins. For example, if a first-time

———————————— oOo ————————————

oOo

author writes a book about a cosmetics company, it is not a hindrance to sales if the author has cooperation and access through e-mail to 20,000 employees. Or, if a first-time author were to produce a book of moderate editorial quality about the benefits of a new, specialized diet, it will help the cause considerably to be a physician or field expert who will be taken seriously by book buyers and the media.

This still does not guarantee success, however. Sen. Trent Lott, R-Mississippi, had his first book published in 2005 by ReganBooks, a very successful division of HarperCollins. Because he has had a long and colorful career and because political books have been the preferred flavor of the past several years, speculation inside the trade was that *Herding Cats* would do very well. As a former senate majority leader, Sen. Lott would certainly have many media opportunities, and people expected long lines of conservatives to buy the book. But again, timing of publication is everything, and just because this book was relatively well-written and contained obvious natural markets, these advantages ultimately did not translate into success.

The launch date was August 25, just four days before Hurricane Katrina hit the Gulf Coast. Sen. Lott, of course, is from Pascagoula, Mississippi, and his home was completely destroyed, as were the book-buying aspirations of hundreds of thousands of people in his natural selling region. Sen. Lott could not and, certainly, would not go on with national media plans talking about his book when his home region had been utterly destroyed. Efforts to revive the campaign months later had less-than-spectacular results, leaving his book in the category unfulfilled expectations. There was nothing to be done

oOo

———————————— oOo ————————————

about it and nobody to blame, but it is yet more proof of how some books deemed good by publishers and the trade never find anticipated success.

For every one, though, there is another book deemed to have less editorial value that steps into its place, selling well in the trade and turning the heads of those who never saw it coming. Professionals in the trade do not like to admit it, but they will readily discuss this fact among themselves, laughing over coffee or drinks at some of the horrendous works that have made bestseller lists and sold hundreds of thousands of copies. Meanwhile, jobs have been lost and careers have been ruined by over-investment and failed promotions of books that editors and publishers believed with all their heart to be of the highest quality and destined to sell thousands of copies.

The lesson for hopeful writers from this is to understand that just because a contract has been secured and a good book has been written and finally published, this does not mean that a long and successful career is in the bag—quite the contrary, considering there are so many other factors that come into play which dictate success. Some, like an unfortunate publication date on 9/11, cannot be avoided, but an author will have more odds stacked in their favor by having paid close attention to marketing and sales plan details from the beginning. My advice is just to expect the worst, preparing as if the book needs all the help it can get.

Write a Good Book, Market it Like a Bad One

At the time of completing this book, I am also working on a Southern humor book under contract for Hill Street Press (www.hillstreetpress.com). For many writers, the career dream

———————————— oOo ————————————

———————————— oOo ————————————

involves reaching a level of experience, which allows you to write the type of book that you want to write, and this is just such a book for me. Dating back to my days as a columnist in Oxford, Mississippi and continuing through my writings for the *Chattanooga Times Free Press*, I have enjoyed, perhaps more than any other type of writing, connecting with people about the places and issues which are intrinsically part of my life. The contract for this book did not include a big advance, but Hill Street is a well-respected house that specializes in quality regional books, and the publisher and editor share a vision with me of opportunity in the marketplace.

I had been carefully pushing my career into a direction that would allow me to write about the subjects I most desired. This step forward in signing the Hill Street Press book was an important culmination of the strategy that began when I first started researching the business of writing. Recognizing that a writer cannot usually write what they want at first, my subjects of concern broadened and evolved accordingly, and I jumped at every opportunity as it came. Discussing Southern issues in a funny-because-it's-true style is a passion beyond almost anything else for me. The single reason I began writing a featured newspaper column for the *Chattanooga Times Free Press*, for instance, was to gain the exposure needed to sign a contract to write this type of book.

Fortunately, the opportunity came along more quickly than I imagined because readers were immediately receptive to my articles, apparently hungry for the dialogue involving such Southern subjects as crystal methamphetamine abuse by women, why blacks and whites do not go to church together

———————————— oOo ————————————

———————————————— oOo ————————————————

and obesity. But, while I believe such an angle for a book fits my writing talents better than perhaps any other, I am not about to sit back and rely on the fact that my book is good to sell. Rather, I will approach it assuming that it needs all of the help it can get and will apply some of the tools that have led not-so-good books to much success.

For instance, I have arranged to send an opt-in e-mail blast—directed to recipients who desire such offers—specifically targeting two million Southerners who fit the demographics of appeal. Using this qualified list, I will offer them something in return for their purchase, like another book—a sort of, "Make this purchase at www.barnesandnoble.com or www.amazon .com on this day and send along your receipt in return, and you will receive other book items valued at more than $50 for free." I have successfully used e-mail blasts to qualified lists before, like on my book about Bill Ford, but I did not take the extra step of offering purchase incentive. As mentioned previously, however, this strategy is working well for authors, and in regard to non-fiction books, at least, it should be used whenever possible.

I am also going to extensively use with promotion of this new book the time-honored methods of marketing, including speaking engagements and market-specific advertisements for this book, believing that once the public is exposed to a new voice of Southern humor, they will warm to it. What I am not going to do is sit back on my proverbial rump and take the attitude that, just because it is well-written and clever and just because a good publishing house that I like and trust has it in print, it will connect with an audience.

There is plenty of proof available, historically speaking, in

———————————————— oOo ————————————————

oOo

the world of publishing to show that, for a variety of reasons, good books often fail from a sales and profit perspective. By marketing the product with the intensity of a not-so-good book, it will have a much better chance of success.

oOo

Chapter 9

The Secrets of Sustainability

When I set forth some years back on a mission of getting published, my objective was not to write one book, but to build a full-time career as an author. I figured there are many stories in this world to tell, and I would be as qualified as anyone to put them in words once I gained necessary experience and knowledge. What I did not fully understand, in my optimism and inexperience, was the difficulty of this proposition. Getting one book published is a significant challenge, but learning the business to the point that a living can actually be earned from the publication of multiple works proves extraordinarily difficult unless you happen to become the next John Grisham or Stephen King your first time at the plate.

This extremely small percentage of ultra-successful authors

oOo

———————————— oOo ————————————

in the industry can get a large contract essentially any moment they produce or promise to produce a new manuscript.
Grisham, for instance, decided to move away from his standard
fiction fare several years ago and his publisher, Doubleday,
never flinched. His books about a football coach, *Bleachers*,
and Christmas, *Skipping Christmas*, were immediate bestsellers.
The rest of us, however, have to work tirelessly just to keep the
paychecks coming and the dream alive, living literally from one
book to the next.

No matter an author's standard of living, the unreliability
of paychecks and the unpredictability of contracts tends to dull
much of what could be a lustrous means of earning a living. One
reason for this is that publishing houses and acquiring editors
usually consider books on an individual basis. Just because *Turnaround*, my first book, sold well in some areas of the world does
not mean that I automatically got another contract and advance.
My experience has been the contrary, in fact, on multiple occasions. Immediately after *Turnaround*, my editor and I discussed a
book based on the fall of once-proud Worldcom and its colorful
founder and CEO Bernie Ebbers. My connections to Ebbers
were strong because of Mississippi roots and my understanding
of his unique personality would have allowed me to write one of
the more interesting books on this corporate saga. The powers-
that-be at HarperBusiness were generally not interested in this
subject, however, and I dropped the concept despite the fact that
my agent and I believed in it. The upside of having pitched it to
HarperCollins, consequently, was that this fulfilled the option
clause in my contract. With their rejection, I was a free agent,
able to shop for a contract with any publishers so desired.

———————————— oOo ————————————

———————————— oOo ————————————

Being a one-hit writer was not of interest, though. Since after selling businesses and leaving employment, writing was to be an occupation, not a hobby. Also, the novelty of having a book published quickly wears off. Even those writers who are gainfully employed and who were not initially seeking a career as an author find that the euphoria of publication is short-lived, and one has the strong desire to seek the experience again.

Be Nimble and Be Quick

My decision after HarperCollins rejected my option proposal was to regroup, but to do so in the shortest means possible. One aspect of publishing a writer quickly learns through hands-on experience is how slow all parts of the industry move. For the impatient, the process can be excruciating. Most publishers, as an example, operate with acquisitions by committee, and because decisions rarely come easily and absentees are common, these deliberations almost always take longer than expected. Once a book is acquired, the execution of contracts and the payment of initial advance checks are just about always a month behind. Then, a manuscript has to be submitted, and publication, all told, requires a minimum of nine months but usually takes twelve or more. Counting the time it takes to gather research and write a proposal, the fastest a writer can expect to move from concept to fruition is a year-and-a-half, and more often it is longer than that.

All of this considered, I recognized that unless I wanted to obtain a full-time job, I needed a viable subject that I could put into action. Fortunately, my experience writing the Carlos Ghosn story had provided me with valuable insight into the

———————————— oOo ————————————

———————— oOo ————————

global automotive industry, and I was very much intrigued by another personality, Ford Motor Company's Bill Ford Jr. Here was America's automaker, nearing its 100th anniversary with the founder of the company's great-grandson at the helm.

Problems abounded as the American car industry suffered through the success of Japanese companies like Toyota, Nissan and Honda. Also, Ford was recovering from the haphazard management of former CEO Jacques Nasser as well as the Explorer/Firestone tire rollover crisis that plagued the company. I believed there was no business story in the world more interesting, considering that Bill Ford Jr. had not been profiled as of yet, and I moved in on the story, obtaining cooperation from needed sources and a contract from a worthy publisher. It was not my desire, admittedly, to write back-to-back automotive books, developing a reputation as "an automotive authority," but the book would be fascinating to write, and it would be another step forward in the effort to build a career.

In writer-speak, this meant, most importantly, that another contract brought another paycheck. Having been previously self-employed for many years, I possessed a broad understanding of the frustrations and difficulties involved with not receiving a regular check to deposit. Still, I was somewhat unprepared for the anemic pattern provided by publishing. For starters, an advance on a book contract is not exactly an advance. In reality, the term advance means guarantee. As an example, if a writer is fortunate to get a $100,000 advance on a book contract, typically $50,000 is paid upon signing, but the publisher will often try to negotiate the rest of the payment in split amounts, perhaps paying another $25,000 upon completion of the work

———————— oOo ————————

———————————————— oOo ————————————————

and another $25,000 at publication—which could be a full two years later.

Making the income situation even more precarious is that many publishers often pay extremely late. Because the industry hovers around booksellers who usually pay their bill 90 days after product delivery, many publishers have adopted notoriously late payment practices. I recall in my contract with HarperCollins that my agent had to make repeated demands for due payments. With three children and too many expenses, the delays in this compensation system made for some long days as the checking account dwindled, desperately needing nourishment. And, of course, once the publisher finally writes the check, it is sent to the agent, sometimes causing another three-week delay.

The idea, certainly, is to save for a rainy day (or months), but this assumes that advance and royalty payments are of a sufficient amount to do so. What works best for me, though, is to work hard and fast, spurring the slow business of publishing along. The process is much like the tapping of a frog on its rear. There is a limit to how fast you can make the frog go, but a series of steady, non-threatening taps will keep it moving.

Sometimes a writer has no choice but to have patience since the right story may not always be available. I was fortunate after my first book to grab onto the untold story of Bill Ford Jr. and Ford Motor Company in its 100th year of business. But there have been other times in which I have been forced to give professional pause, waiting for the right story to emerge. The best example of this was right after I finished writing *The John Deere Way* and *Endurance: Winning Life's Majors The Phil Mickelson Way* at the end of 2004. Several interesting potential subjects

———————————————— oOo ————————————————

oOo

had come my way via my worthy agent Frank Weimann, including the Maloof brothers, owners of the NBA's Sacremento Kings and The Palms Casino, who have an interesting story to tell of customer service, or the five-time world boxing champion, Vinnie Paz. Known in the ring as the Pazmanian Devil, this man is the real-life Rocky, having come back from a broken neck to win his last title. I was fortunate to get to know both the Maloof brothers and Mr. Paz in consideration of these projects, and while I think they will come to fruition in the future, the timing for neither was at that moment.

I also considered writing a book about how legendary Ford Motor Company founder Henry Ford essentially gave birth to the soybean as we know it in the 21st century world. Known for his obsessive qualities of exploration, Mr. Ford became intrigued with the concept of chemurgy — the making of industrial products from raw agricultural materials — in the 1920s, focusing his efforts on the soybean, which had been used in a handful of culinary ways in Asia for thousands of years but was a relatively unknown entity in North America.

Despite there having been less than 10 million acres of soybean in annual production in the United States at the time, Mr. Ford ordered his in-house scientists to study and find any and all possible food and industrial uses for the soybean. His notion was that the product would change the world, feeding the hungry and serving as a base component in such products as cars through its use in plastics and paints. So sold on the soybean was Mr. Ford that he featured the legume at a World's Fair, treating journalists to a full-course soybean meal. He ordered his company to build a car made out of a plastic derived from

oOo

————————————————— oOo —————————————————

soybeans, and he wore around a somewhat itchy suit that was woven with soy fibers.

Many people, including some major media types of the time, laughed at Mr. Ford's strange conviction that the soybean would become the answer to sustainable manufacturing and food production; but, within 10 years, production of the crop in the United States had increased tenfold. Today, there are literally hundreds of everyday uses for the soybean, from paint to imitation meat, and most trace back to patents and work done by Mr. Ford's scientists.

I became familiar with the story through time spent in Dearborn, Michigan while researching the Bill Ford Jr. book. In spare time, I would pass hours at The Henry Ford museum, learning much in amazement about this unique story of invention and aspiration. Realizing that no significant book about the subject had been written, I put together a worthy proposal (*see appendix B*), and Mr. Weimann went about selling it. The problem was many editors felt the several dozen of books already written about Mr. Ford weakened the subject matter, making the book a hard sell in the trade.

Frankly, I had a hard time disagreeing, and even though we had some interest, we decided to kill the project and move along to more profitable concepts. Abandoning a project can be difficult for a writer, however, because they have often become attached to the subject and starting over also means more months without a paycheck. But the ability to be flexible as well as the ability to make decisions quickly and decisively are necessities if you plan to earn enough money writing books to make it a career.

————————————————— oOo —————————————————

оОо

Respect the Rules, but Always Maintain Creativity

The intricacies of individualism apply to publishing, just as they do for people in any business. As stated throughout this book, the secret to first getting published is to learn the rules and generally abide by them so that the doors of agents and editors will open for you, not close. It is a highly structured wall that has been built to keep the uniformed and unprepared out. If you want in, learning the business is most often imperative. However, once you have crossed the transom and become a published author, the objective shifts to sustainability.

For this to occur, a slippery slope must be traversed between rules of the trade and personal style. As an example, one of my strengths is deal-making. I enjoy the chasing, negotiation and closing of a deal. Therefore, I tend to be heavily involved on front-end talks with editors. Additionally, I enjoy the business of publishing, and remaining in close contact keeps me abreast of trends in the industry. For some authors, such an up-close-and-personal relationship might be a disaster, with their personality getting in the way of good and worthy projects. Typically, editors do not want authors that close, preferring instead to have all discussions with the agent. But it works for me, and I often approach projects in this way to gain front-end feedback and to eliminate the wasting of time even though rules of the game suggest it is a bad idea.

My agent, fortunately, recognizes my style and allows me freedoms without stepping on my toes, and editors are likewise free to discuss potential projects and share thoughts. Also, in other areas I yield heavily to my agent whereas some authors may not. I never start on a project, for example, without having

оОо

———————— oOo ————————

his blessing because I value his insight and experience. Similarly, I typically discuss project concepts with my wife, who also has a keen sense for trends and tastes. If I get thumbs up from these trusted allies, my process is to then play the potential project off some editor contacts and friends in the business to further determine viability before spending valuable time researching for and writing a proposal. The point is worth reiterating, however, that there are no guarantees in the business of writing, and for an author to maintain sustainability, one must work to obtain recurring contracts from publishers and to continually reach bookseller shelves around the country and world with new product—all by engaging in a blend of considerate rule-playing combined with personal style and creativity.

This can be a sometimes slippery slope that poses as a difficulty for authors to walk. Publishing has been a balancing act for me, and if you are able cross the transom, I have no doubt it will be for you as well. The business of writing can be conquered, though, if the trade is properly learned and its key secrets to success are mastered. The reward is a career that has no equals in terms of enjoyment, satisfaction and reward, making the path worth taking if you feel confident you possess writing talent, creativity, respect for tradition, and, above all, patience.

———————— oOo ————————

Appendix A

Author's Note: This slightly edited copy of a proposal, my first, was sold in 2002 to HarperCollins by my agent at the time, Elizabeth Frost-Knappman of New England Publishing Associates. The deal was for six figures and offers were made from multiple publishers. The book was published as *Turnaround: How Carlos Ghosn Rescued Nissan 2003* and has since sold more than 100,000 copies worldwide in seven languages. Selling strengths of the proposal, my publisher later told me, included a crisp and riveting overview and strong chapter title headings, showing action.

oOo

——— oOo ———

How Carlos Ghosn Rescued Nissan
by David Magee

Overview

When French automaker Renault acquired control of Japan's beleaguered automaker Nissan, global observers predicted a disastrous clash of cultures. The predictions of doom became more ominous when the announcement was made that a 46-year-old, fiery Brazilian would take over the Japanese corporate giant.

The book *How Carlos Ghosn Rescued Nissan* will be a serious look at the business strategy and personality of the man who has arguably become the world's most successful CEO in just a few years by turning around Japan's No. 2 automaker.

It will detail how Ghosn learned his authoritative leadership style, beginning with his days growing up in Brazil and learning to speak more than five languages fluently; to his earning the nickname "the killer" at Michelin North America and later Renault for aggressive cost-cutting measures as president and executive vice president; to the day the business community was shocked when Ghosn became the first westerner to head Nissan.

Ghosn's personality is displayed in the book through a tight explanation of his cutting-edge management strategies and unwavering principles, ideals that have been carefully crafted through years of instinctual observation. The book details how Ghosn pushed Renault executives to take stake in what many believed a hopeless cause.

"If Nissan is not in the black within one year, I will resign," Ghosn said after accepting the job as Nissan president and chief operating officer.

——— oOo ———

oOo

Ghosn, who now has the title CEO, is a man who never speaks without careful thought. The book follows Ghosn's words closely, unveiling his no-fail style to a reading world hungry for a fresh corporate icon.

The Nissan Revival Plan (NRP) Ghosn unveiled in 1999 was aggressive beyond reason, but those close to him believed in the plan's success, just as they believed he would truly quit in a year if Nissan didn't float in the black.

The plan's numbers were staggering. Ghosn trimmed the workforce by 14 percent, shutting down five plants. The number of companies supplying Nissan was cut in half, ending many cozy Japanese corporate relationships — keiretsu — in existence for years. The results, however, are staggering as well. Nissan posted a $1.56 billion profit for six months ending September 2001 — up 39 percent from the previous year.

Ghosn's heavy-handed tactics reinforced his nickname "the killer" in Japan, but though jobs have been lost and long-time relationships severed, his revitalization plan relies more on forward-thinking advances than a wake of destruction. For each stone Ghosn leaves crumbled in his wake, five more are cast forward as future foundation for Nissan.

How Carlos Ghosn Rescued Nissan tells the story of the man who cut costs as expected. Ghosn, after all, was heavily involved as Renault executive vice president in a controversial move by the company to shut down its plant in Belgium. That Ghosn would cut costs at Nissan was a secret to few; that his plan for the future would be so focused has caught some in the automotive world off guard.

Ghosn said when announcing the revival plan that Nissan

oOo

cannot "save its way to success" and rolled the dice on major investments, including new products and new plants. Well calculated, but high in risk, he pushed the company to launch 13 new models by 2002 and build needed infrastructure to facilitate the process.

The business world is taking notice, but the people paying the closest attention are the ones in his midst, the Japanese citizens many observers thought the Brazilian stood no chance with.

The book will closely describe the tactics Ghosn has used to earn the trust of the Japanese—he came to the country with a "clean sheet of paper" and no stereotypes and "listened to the people"—and includes first-hand interviews and observations from Tokyo.

Nissan won't complete its revival plan until 2003, but immediate measurable results, combined with a bold savvy and uncanny ability to study and listen have perched Ghosn atop the heap in a day when most global CEOs have asked for too much and delivered too little.

The book *How Carlos Ghosn Rescued Nissan* will tell this story…about how a Brazilian emerged as a global business leader and hero in a land where many believed he did not belong.

Market Analysis
No book has been written about Carlos Ghosn, the man quickly becoming the world's top CEO, thus creating a global market for *How Carlos Ghosn Rescued Nissan*.

Books about management styles of current and former CEOs continue to sell well, evidenced by Lee Iacocca's 1986 autobiography, which today is still among the top books sold

———————————— oOo ————————————

at Amazon.com, some fifteen years after publication. Additionally, *Guts: The Seven Laws of Business That Made Chrysler the World's Hottest Car Company* by Robert A. Lutz John A. Wiley and Sons, 1998) is still among the top 15,000 sellers at Amazon.com.

Carlos Ghosn's story is more compelling globally than Iacocca's was before or Jack Welch's is now because Ghosn is a Brazilian who lived for years in Greenville, South Carolina, while helping turn around tire company Michelin North America; became a well-known figure in France by pushing for publicized cost-cutting measures during Renault's turnaround; and is a celebrity-type figure in Japan after shaking up Nissan.

Simply, the fascination inspired by Carlos Ghosn goes far beyond the United States. The book, in fact, may find its strongest markets outside the U.S.

How Carlos Ghosn Rescued Nissan will be published at the time Ghosn will likely be the most sought-after CEO in the corporate world. Ghosn is no secret in automotive circles today, but has maintained a relatively low profile, choosing to let products speak for Nissan. The secret, however, is getting out.

"He could write his own ticket," a London-based industry analyst said last year. The analyst went on to say that Ghosn would add $10 billion overnight to DaimlerChrysler's market capitalization if he were named that company's CEO.

The book has market appeal because it tells the story of an innovative business leader who reached far beyond a typical CEO's comfort zone, rescuing a dying company through aggressive measures and opening up a traditionally closed Japanese landscape.

———————————— oOo ————————————

—————————— oOo ——————————

Approach

How Carlos Ghosn Rescued Nissan will be a 60,000-word book targeted to people who read books about innovative business management techniques and/or success stories about global integration of people and ideas.

The book will follow the cultural challenges Ghosn faced while rebuilding Japan's No. 2 automaker, creating a readability and interest rarely seen in business books.

How Carlos Ghosn Rescued Nissan will follow the path of events, starting with Ghosn's insistence to fellow Renault executives that taking control in Nissan was a gamble worth taking, while detailing Ghosn's no-fail management style.

How Carlos Ghosn Rescued Nissan will have an endearing slant on the union between the people of Japan and Ghosn, detailing his efforts to earn their trust and their respect for his hard-line approach.

It will also include interviews of former employees of Nissan plants in Japan that Ghosn shut down—these people worked hard and methodically until the very last car rolled off the assembly line—and it will include first-hand accounts of days in the life of Carlos Ghosn in Tokyo, providing the reader an in-depth look into his decision-making processes.

The story will be told in journalistic-style, adding personality and culture to a story based on numbers.

About the Author

David Magee is a public relations executive and former newspaper editor with a passion for business stories with flair in a world where most are stale and predictable.

—————————— oOo ——————————

———————————— oOo ————————————

Magee is a vice president for one of the largest advertising and marketing firms in the Southeast and was formerly news editor and columnist of two daily community newspapers. Magee and Ghosn developed a relationship when Ghosn was in Mississippi announcing Nissan's new plant in 2001.

Magee is a freelance writer and has been a regular contributing writer for the Associated Press (college basketball), the Jackson MS *Clarion-Ledger* (business) and the *Oxford* (MS) *Eagle*.

He was named to the *Mississippi Business Journal's* **Top 40 Under 40** in Mississippi in 1998; was named one of the state's top newspaper columnists in 1993 by the Mississippi Press Association; and has been elected to public office two times.

Magee is also the founder of Jefferson Press, a new publishing house focusing on creative Southern works.

The Carlos Ghosn File

Carlos Ghosn is Chief Executive Officer of Nissan Motor Corp., Ltd. and a member of the company's Board of Directors. Ghosn joined Nissan in June 1999.

He previously was Executive Vice President of Renault, in charge of general management and President and Chief Operating Officer of Michelin North America.

At Michelin, Ghosn negotiated the merger between Michelin North America and Uniroyal Goodrich Tire Co. and assimilated and developed the multi-brand strategy of Michelin North America after its acquisition.

Ghosn was born in Brazil—he is Lebanese by descent, Brazilian by birth, a French citizen and Japanese by adoption,

———————————— oOo ————————————

———————————————— oOo ————————————————

is how Ghosn puts it—and holds engineering degrees from the Ecole Polytechnique and the Ecole des Mines de Paris. He is married and has three daughters and a son.

Ghosn was listed by *Business Week* magazine in 2001 among the Top 25 Managers in the world.

The article said "Carlos Ghosn, the troubleshooter charged with reviving Nissan Motor Co., likes to be called the "Icebreaker." It's a nickname he got from DaimlerChrysler Chairman Jurgen E. Schrempp for his skill at ignoring local business practices that stand in the way of making money.

Chapter Outline

Chapter One

The reader will be introduced to Carlos Ghosn and Nissan by portraying events surrounding the 2001 groundbreaking for the company's new plant in Mississippi. This broad overview will provide insight into Ghosn's personality and Nissan's rebuilding challenge, drawing the reader into the intricate story of how Ghosn developed a plan to revitalize the company and executed it on cue.

It will also remind the reader of Nissan's storied past, about how the company changed became a global business force with its sleek products, including the popular Z car, once known as the fastest selling sports car of its time, and was a major factor in the struggle of American automakers in the latter part of the 20th century.

Chapter One tells the reader how Nissan got into trouble in recent years and shows Ghosn's willingness, as the company's

———————————————— oOo ————————————————

chosen savior, to do the unexpected in efforts to turn Nissan around.

Chapter Two

Carlos Ghosn, a married father of four, was born in Brazil and educated in France at the finest engineering universities in the country. This chapter will tell Ghosn's family background and offer insight from first-hand interviews about the man's early driving forces. He has a relentless energy that keeps those around him focused, including his family. He's a taskmaster who expects every question to have an honest answer. Excuses are out of the question.

Chapter Three

Ghosn is introduced to the corporate world in 1978 when he joins tire-maker Michelin in France. He holds a variety of positions in manufacturing plants and the company's development center. He is promoted to plant manager in 1981 and by 1986 has advanced to chief operating officer of Michelin South America.

Chapter Three tells the reader how Ghosn became president and chief operating officer of Michelin North America, headquartered in Greenville, South Carolina, in 1989 and negotiated the highly publicized merger between his company and Uniroyal Goodrich Tire Company. Ghosn, as chairman, president and chief executive officer of the new Michelin North America, effectively assimilates the companies and develops and implements a successful multi-brand strategy for Michelin and Uniroyal Goodrich tires.

Chapter Four
Ghosn joins France's Renault Motor in October 1996 when he feels his job at Michelin is complete and is named executive vice president in charge of general management, responsible for advanced research, purchasing, vehicle engineering and development, power train operations and the MERCOSUR business unit in Latin America.

Chapter Four tells how Ghosn once again creates change for a company when he pushes Renault to close its plant in Belgium amid high publicity and protests against the action. The move, however, was crucial to Renault's renewed success and helped the company dramatically reverse its fortunes.

Chapter Five
Nissan Motors is struggling in Japan and rumors of bankruptcy are circulating in the automotive industry. The company can find no help in Japan as most of the business community is already intertwined with the country's No. 2 automaker. Most outsiders aren't even considering the daunting task of taking over the giant buried deeply in Japanese business traditions.

Renault's Ghosn sees it differently and pushes his company to acquire a 37 percent stake in Nissan. A few short months later Ghosn is named president and chief operating officer, becoming the first westerner to lead Nissan. More than a few heads are turned and predictions of doom are more than hushed whispers.

Chapter Six
When Ghosn moves to Tokyo in June 1999 and takes over Nissan he has been a corporate leader for more than 20 years, yet

——————————————— oOo ———————————————

he proclaims from day one he has come to Japan with "a clean sheet of paper" and an open mind to the company's needs.

He tells all: "I have come to Japan for the good of Nissan, not for the good of Renault."

This chapter will be a "state of the union" at Nissan when Ghosn first arrived and it will discuss the business skills Ghosn has developed and how he used them to assess Nissan and it will discuss Ghosn's excitement about the challenge of leading Nissan.

"At Michelin and Renault I was mainly part of a team focusing on the revival of a company," Ghosn said. "This is the first time I am in charge, with total responsibility. There are more things at stake and more responsibility."

Chapter Seven
Everyone knew Carlos Ghosn would cut costs at Nissan. The company was losing millions of dollars each month, had more than $20 billion in debt and a man nicknamed "the killer" was now in charge. The questions about Ghosn were whether the Brazilian would be accepted by the Japanese, and vice versa.

But Ghosn had a plan, as outlined in this chapter. He would go to the country with no preconceived ideas about the people and learn their ways and culture first-hand.

"I had to erase what I thought I knew about the country and start from zero," Ghosn said. "When you go to a country that is not your own you have to be prepared to live and adapt to that country. It should be an enjoyable experience and a learning one."

Ghosn began learning Japanese and integrated himself and

——————————————— oOo ———————————————

his family into Tokyo despite the fact that he's considered a celebrity in the country and needs escorts to get from one point to another.

Chapter Eight

Ghosn's paper didn't stay blank for long. He listened, observed and studied for five months. Then, he unveiled arguably the most aggressive and long term revival plan a global corporation has ever seen. The Nissan Revival Plan (NRP), announced in October 1999, was designed by Ghosn to achieve immediate and lasting profitable growth for Nissan worldwide.

The highlights of the three-year plan are detailed in this chapter. They include:

- Massive cost cutting. Five plants are closed, more than 21,000 jobs eliminated.
- New product launches. More than 22 brand new models will be launched.
- Major emphasis on U.S. market. Ghosn says Nissan was far from its potential in America and says more money will be invested in developing the market.
- Reduced purchasing costs. Ghosn challenges Japan's keiretsu, the long-standing tradition in Japan where corporations buy from each other at inflated costs, and pushes Nissan to purchase globally.

Chapter Nine

Five plants close in Japan, a direct result of the revival plan. Ghosn is amazed at the last-minute work ethic of those losing jobs.

—— oOo ——

"The involvement, the loyalty, the intensity that Japanese) show for their company is amazing," Ghosn said.

Workers remained committed to jobs until the last car rolled off each line. Ghosn faced challenges from a few during this period including some from the old-boy network that ran Nissan for years and those issues are documented in this chapter, including Ghosn's handling of the situation.

Nissan implements a system that rewards merit, not seniority. Ghosn also announces a stock option plan, unheard of in a country where large bonuses to senior managers are the norm.

The chapter talks about challenges Ghosn is facing from Japanese traditionalists, including groups such as the Japan Auto Parts Industries Association, which has publicly and privately rebuked Ghosn and his outside management techniques.

"I'm not saying everybody appreciates all the measures we have taken," Ghosn said.

Chapter Ten

Ghosn knew he was taking drastic measures in the turnaround effort and needed quick results for employee and stockholder buy-in.

The early numbers are staggering. Nissan's profits have risen, posting a dramatic turnaround in just one year that brings the company back from collapse. Profits for the six-month period ending September 2000 are $1.2 billion, the best numbers posted in more than a decade.

"We had to show quick victories to accelerate the number of people buying into our plan," Ghosn said.

Ghosn predicts Nissan will enjoy a full year of profitability

—— oOo ——

in 2001 and sales in the U.S. will increase by double digits, a meaningful statement considering Ford, General Motors and Chrysler saw sales declines in the short term.

This chapter reveals Nissan's improved results, casting them against Ghosn's revival plan, and discusses the future between Renault and Nissan the exact stake is still being determined.)

Chapter Eleven
"He's Z Man: Brazilian boss Carlos Ghosn is hoping a re-launched Z car will resuscitate Nissan."

The headline appearing in Time Magazine's Asia edition echoed sentiments of observers of the auto industry in 2001. Ghosn, clearly, is the man and all eyes are on him at the Detroit Auto Show when the veil is taken off the much-anticipated Z car Nissan is launching.

The product, designed by Shiro Nakamura, is a direct result of Ghosn's aggressive style. Ghosn hired Nakamura away from Isuzu in 1999 and charged him immediately with leading the most complex phase of Nissan's revival: new product representing innovation representative of the company's past.

Chapter Eleven discusses each of Nissan's new products, from the revamped Infiniti line, to the new Z car and brisk-selling Xterra.

Chapter Twelve
Nissan is on the right track but Ghosn is relentless, a tireless work committed to the revival plan every minute of every day. The intense, bespectacled Brazilian knows cost cutting has saved Nissan, but only superior product and intense focus will

make the company a leading global car company for the long term.

He continues to push hard, working 16-hour days and demanding strong results from every division under the Nissan umbrella.

The chapter follows stories of Ghosn's demanding management style.

He visits a dealer manager, speaking with him through an ever-present interpreter: "Your results show a loss. We want to know first, why? And second, what are you going to do about it?"

The manager stammers. Ghosn is irritated, shakes his head and snaps.

"This is your responsibility. Brainstorm. Discuss. You will be held responsible."

Chapter Thirteen

The harder Ghosn pushes, the bigger his legend grows in Japan. Doubters believed a westerner would face revolt in Japan, but Chapter Thirteen tells how Ghosn has become an icon in a country hungry for corporate romance.

Corporate leaders use "*Ghosn-san*" as a reference in discussions about improving other Japanese businesses and housewives croon over the man some say is Japan's sexiest. One woman watched a television interview with Ghosn and was speechless.

"I had never felt so moved," she said. Why? "His management reforms."

When Ghosn travels in the country it is with entourage as protection from citizens eager to see and touch their new icon.

———————————————— oOo ————————————————

The chapter also quotes global leaders who tell how Ghosn has opened the door to westerners wanting and needing to conduct business in Japan circles that have long been closed to outsiders.

Chapter Fourteen

Nissan's plan isn't complete until the end of 2002 and challenges lie ahead. An adverse economy has altered forecasts and the company's stock has slumped over speculation that a stronger Nissan will in turn take a stake in Renault.

Chapter Fourteen discusses these issues critical to a complete execution of Ghosn's plan, but reiterates that recent victories have already assured that Nissan is once again a global automotive force. The revival plan is summarized and data are concluded here.

Chapter Fifteen

Ghosn's efforts at Nissan have made him arguably the world's most successful CEO in just a few short years. The final chapter looks at Ghosn's successes in a broad glance, reminding the reader the daunting task he has completed: Taking over a failing Japanese corporate giant as an outsider and deliver remarkable results in a short period while captivating the country's people.

Ghosn says he will not leave Nissan until he's "not needed anymore" and the chapter will analyze when that will be and what may be next for Carlos Ghosn.

———————————————— oOo ————————————————

oOo

Sample Writing

Chapter One

Every few minutes another bus emerges from a dust cloud and stops, unloading dignitaries by the dozens. They are all dressed the same. Men in blue suits, women in high heels. But they are different. Some are black; some white; others, Japanese, creating a cultural mix rarely seen in these parts in large numbers. It's a sunny spring day in rural Canton, Mississippi and hundreds have come to hear the words of a fiery, intellectual Brazilian, Carlos Ghosn.

Nissan Motors is breaking ground for its new $930 million North American manufacturing plant, an integral part of the revival plan designed to return the once-struggling company to greatness. Ghosn, the company's president and chief operating officer, is on hand for the honors. So are all the other dignitaries one would expect for such an event, including Mississippi Senator Trent Lott, who earned Ghosn's trust and was a leading factor in the plant-location decision. It's a moment of celebration for Mississippi, a state normally on the bottom of everything in America: lowest per capita income, highest rate of illiteracy.

Mississippi has seen better times recently, thanks to money flowing from water-based gambling that was approved by the state legislature ten years earlier. In 1998 Mississippi even eclipsed New Jersey, becoming the country's second largest gambling state behind Nevada, but few noticed. There are other successes. World Com, based in Clinton, became a telecommunications giant as Bernie Ebbers engineered a string of leveraged acquisitions that inflated stock portfolios throughout the sparsely populated

oOo

— oOo —

state and created thousands of higher-paying jobs. Mississippi was also the place that made tobacco companies cry uncle, making a handful of the state's lawyers—including Lott's brother in law—rich.

Still, most of the attention given to Mississippi goes to other things, like the past, or the high infant mortality rate or the Confederate stars and bars that still adorn the state flag. It is a proud place, to be sure, but one that rarely celebrates victory over other states, much less its Southern neighbors. Tennessee landed Saturn in Spring Hill and Nissan in Smyrna; Alabama got Mercedes-Benz in Vance.

Mississippi Gov. Ronnie Musgrove told Nissan officials seeking a North American plant location in 2000 it was his state's turn to land an automaker. He solicited help from Lott and persuaded the state's legislature to offer incentives so rich Nissan couldn't say no. Canton is one of the poorer towns in one of the poorer states, but its proximity to Jackson—just 20 miles to the North—and Interstate 55 apparently made the predominantly black town a natural for Nissan.

So here is Ghosn, waiting at the groundbreaking ceremony for everyone to arrive, about to dig a hole in Mississippi and bury a billion dollars in it.

Another bus makes it way toward the tent, driving through the middle of hundreds of acres of barren dirt, already bulldozed in site preparation. Spring winds are causing a dust storm, but protestors line the final, unsecured leg of the entrance nonetheless, covering their faces with shirtsleeves to escape the dust. One group, all white, waves Confederate battle flags to passers-by. Another group, all black, holds a "new" state

— oOo —

flag. Mississippi is about to take a statewide vote on adopting a new flag, minus the Confederate stars and bars that adorn the current one. Polls show the anticipated vote runs deeply down racial lines and conventional wisdom says the new look has no chance of passing. Almost forty years have passed since James Meredith integrated Ole Miss, Mississippi's flagship university, to the dismay of then-Governor Ross Barnett and thousands of citizens who protested his federally mandated enrollment. More than 1,000 African American students attend the university today and bars of racial harmony are being sung from top to bottom. But the flag—tradition—must stay the same.

Ghosn isn't happy about the raging debate or the anticipated outcome. Nissan has been embroiled in a much-publicized class action lawsuit alleging the company practiced unfair lending with minorities trying to buy cars and wants no part in Mississippi's racial struggles. But the sun is bright and temperature cool inside the big-top tent on this day and a diverse group is assembling inside to watch the Brazilian announce the coming of a Japanese corporation to Mississippi.

The all-black Canton High School band plays the national anthem. A Japanese drum corps stirs the crowd and reminds all that Nissan is still steeped in its home-country's tradition. A nearby resident tells a newspaper reporter about the event: "It's a blessing from God." It's also unity, except the flag-bearers standing near the entrance.

Ghosn speaks. He talks about Nissan's revival efforts and affirms the company's return to profitability for a full fiscal year, a far cry from the bankruptcy it faced two years earlier.

—— oOo ——

He says Nissan will employ thousands at the Mississippi plant and make new products, giving the company a bright future in America.

A black lady wearing a Sunday dress is half-seated on a table at the rear of the tent and waving her arms. She punctuates every word of emphasis and pause from Ghosn loud and clear with words of thanksgiving. *"Praise God."*

For Mississippi, it's an Amen day. Four thousand high-wage jobs, a billion dollar investment…unity. For Nissan and Ghosn, it's the parlay play of an aggressive revival plan designed to return Nissan to its position as one of the most respected and in some circles) feared automakers in the world.

Nissan was established in Japan in 1933 and made a major impact on the global auto market in the late 1950s when it first introduced its Datsun-brand sedans and compact pickup trucks to the United States. It was a risky move, observers felt, coming so soon after the World War II when emotions toward the Japanese still ran high, but the products didn't appeal to older Americans anyway. The sports cars were sleek and exactly what the younger, faster generation wanted. The 2000 Roadster, with its five-speed, 150 horsepower engine, was first produced in 1967, establishing the Datsun brand for its unique European style and Japanese performance.

The company experienced dramatic growth in the 1970s when its popular Z model was introduced. The 240Z became the fastest selling sports car in the world, selling more than 500,000 units in fewer than ten years. The long-nosed rocket car, desired by teenagers and twenty something's across America, helped push Nissan's other Datsun products to popularity as

—— oOo ——

well, positioning the brand in America as one with unequaled performance, engineering and value.

By 1975 Datsun was the top U.S. vehicle importer and Nissan's Japanese style of business was well documented—and envied—throughout the world, particularly in the United States where General Motors and Chrysler struggled with antiquated management, too slow to react to the invigorated, fast-moving Japanese.

Nissan built its first American plant in Smyrna, Tennessee in the early 1980s and began marketing all of its vehicles world-wide under the Nissan name at the same time. Nissan launched its luxury Infiniti line in the early 1990s to acclaim and soared in North America and around the world to the delight of the all-Japanese upper level management team still in place.

But problems began to develop in the mid to late 1990s, about the time Nissan killed production of its once-popular Z car. Management that was once hailed as progressive and trend setting was now a part of Japan's old-boy network, arrogant and oblivious to market changes and customer needs. Top Japanese companies were tied together through traditional supplier relationships—keiretsu, a system of cross holding of stocks that was devised during the country's rapid economic growth in the 1950s and 1960s. Typically, 30 to 50 percent of stocks were cross-held by companies in the same keiretsu as a means of preventing takeovers by outside investors.

In sectors such as automobile manufacturing, this process fostered long-term relationships between buyers and suppliers, as keiretsu members jointly worked together on product development. Nissan was deeply tied into this process as senior management felt obligated to buy from partners in its Fuyo group, typically at a premium. Simply, suppliers over time had raised prices to the point Tokyo-based Nissan could no longer survive. Former Nissan Chairman Yoshifumi Tsuji admitted in 1999 the company's problems were far worse than anticipated.

"Until a few years ago, holding large liabilities with interest in Japan was not necessarily viewed as a problem," Tsuji said.

Views, though, changed and the fact that Nissan was in dire straits was a secret to none, but nobody in Japan had a solution as it was considered taboo in the country for these keiretsu links to be broken. Eventually Nissan was strapped by $22 billion in debt, inflated supplier costs and new product development that was at a standstill. Nobody in Japan had an answer and once-generous financiers were tightening the noose on the company. Nissan was on the brink of bankruptcy, its stock price drifting to low single digits, and it was on the sale block, but the phone wasn't ringing since most outsiders thought foreigners stood no chance rebuilding a company in Japan with western tactics and personnel.

Ghosn and his fellow leaders at Renault—namely CEO Louis Schweitzer—having successfully turned around the French auto maker in the mid 1990s, sensed desperation in Japan and believed, faced with no options, powers-that-be in the country would not oppose foreign capital taking over the company regarded by many to be the centerpiece of Japan's post-war industrial success.

They couldn't have been more right. The Ministry of International Trade and Industry MITI), the powerhouse of the Japanese economy, publicly blessed the move and public sentiment in Japan was calm, even welcoming.

—— ∘O∘ ——

"A lot of things characterize the Japanese people," Ghosn said. "We can debate them. But one characteristic we cannot debate is that they are very pragmatic. They are also very sensitive to reality. And the reality of Nissan was not hidden. It was crystal clear. Something had to be done."

Ghosn is in a restaurant in Oxford, Mississippi having a promised four-star meal at a noted eatery the day after the groundbreaking ceremony for Nissan's new North American plant. The mood is casual, a short rest after a grueling tour of the States that began in a Washington meeting with Senator Trent Lott and culminated in Canton for the groundbreaking.

It's Saturday in the college town and Ghosn is wearing an open collared shirt; his wife, who is accompanying him, jeans. Advance notice was clear: Ghosn *does not want to talk business.* He just wants to see that state and people his company is now doing business in.

The head of Japan's No. 2 automaker is seated at the table with his wife; Nissan Vice President for North American operations, Jim Morton, and his wife; a Nissan public relations assistant; and two new acquaintances. Conversation is light, covering topics from the poorly decorated Governor's Mansion in Mississippi, to the best places in the world to eat and travel. The 46-year-old Ghosn is a Brazilian globaliste who has traveled extensively as an upper level corporate executive, drawing his paycheck in three different countries the last six years. Ghosn likes Rio and Paris and Greenville, South Carolina; places he has lived. He dislikes airports and the inconsistencies in getting there, like any executive worth his weight in stock options.

—— ∘O∘ ——

————————————— oOo —————————————

Ghosn wants a beer. He's disappointed by the muted selections the young waitress offers, but finds a selection that will do.

He pours the beer in a glass and nurses it slowly. Food is served. Ghosn takes a bite and pauses. He looks at his wife and mumbles in French.

"C'est terrible."

Translation: This is awful.

An acquaintance snickers, catching the barb. Ghosn shrugs and pushes his plate away, turning to his new acquaintance. "Tell me what you think about Nissan," he says.

It's all business now. Ghosn has no interest in the meal that doesn't meet expectation and begins a series of short, calculated questions to new acquaintances. He hangs on every word in response, searching past flattery for his sake for slivers of truth. An opening of "I love Nissan…I'm on my second Maxima" turns into: My friends don't shop Nissan, probably, because "the product line is too limited" for their taste.

Ghosn does not speak until every word of each answer to every question falls off the tongue of his acquaintances. He wants input on everything from the functionality of Nissan's new-fangled Maxima to impressions of Yates Construction, the Mississippi-based company selected to build the company's billion-dollar plant in impoverished Canton. There's no better company to *build* the plant, he's told. Yates is one of the top 50 construction firms in America and company president Bill Yates is a hands-on detail man known to stick to budget. The public relations aspect is different. Yates is based in Philadelphia, Mississippi, a town as noted for its civil rights struggles as the entire state of Mississippi. And Yates is not a company

————————————— oOo —————————————

—————————————— oOo ——————————————

necessarily known for its compassion toward minorities, Ghosn is told.

He's heard it before, no doubt, but furrows his brow when hearing it again.

"Like I said. We have many challenges."

The mood is light again, almost playful now that expectations have been removed and Ghosn has dissected the psyche of all in his midst and received honest answers on sensitive subjects. Questions come back at him now and he plays the game, firing short answers in rapid-fire urgency.

Acquaintance: "Do you like Japan?"

Ghosn, smiling: "Yes."

Acquaintance: "What do you think about Mississippi?"

Ghosn: "I like it very much. The people here are very friendly and they want to make this work."

Acquaintance: "What has happened to Xerox? Talk about needing a new plan."

Ghosn: "Top level management sat by and watched that company crumble."

Acquaintance: "What do you think about corporate management in general right now?"

Pause.

Ghosn: "C'est terrible."

It is obvious Ghosn is making a joke, but the point is not missed. There are pockets of good, he says, backing up his French with an English explanation. But they are getting fewer and farther between.

And, if anybody knows mismanagement, it's Carlos Ghosn. Each company he's worked for has been a textbook study in

—————————————— oOo ——————————————

——————————————— oOo ———————————————

corporate misdirection and confusion when he arrived...Michelin North America, French automaker Renault and now, Nissan. He was president of Michelin North America, engineering that company's merger with Uniroyal Goodrich, and executive vice president of Renault, pushing for massive cost cutting measures during that company's restructuring.

But in 1999, when Ghosn was named Nissan's President — the CEO title was awarded in 2001 — the challenge was monumental to what he faced as leader-apprentice at Michelin North America and Renault. Nissan was about to go under and the challenge, ultimately, is now all his.

When Renault's Schweitzer announced in March 1999 his company was taking a 37 percent stake in Nissan for $5.6 billion and three months later that Ghosn would take charge of the struggling company, more than a few in the global business community were shocked. It was one thing for Renault to take control of Nissan; another altogether for an outsider to be sent in so quickly. Few questioned whether a hardliner like Ghosn could create change at Nissan. They wondered if a westerner would face crippling hostility and revolt from Japanese accustomed to a bureaucratic and slow-moving style steeped in deep tradition of techniques once revered by business gurus everywhere. Simply, the business challenge was one thing; the cultural challenge another.

Even if the people are accepting in the beginning, how will they react to massive changes? Ghosn earned the nickname "le killer" in France for his drastic cost-cutting recommendations at Renault. It was no secret Ghosn was the driving force behind Renault's controversial decision in the late 1990s to close a major manufacturing plant in Belgium. The Japanese economy was in

——————————————— oOo ———————————————

bad shape already and plant closings there certainly would be met with revolt, a bruising local effort to put Ghosn in his rightful place—out of Japan.

Ghosn, however, arrived in Japan with an attitude oblivious to tradition and rolled the dice with his aggressive Nissan Revival Plan NRP), announced in late 1999. The plan was detailed and far reaching, but perhaps the most importance is placed in Mississippi: A billion-dollar investment for a new plant designed to manufacture full-size trucks and sleek new mini-vans. Thus, the reason Ghosn wants to see, experience and understand the state that before Nissan's announcement listed its biggest business coup as the addition of gambling.

Granted, it's just one plant, but every move Ghosn has made to date has been geared at short-term survival and long-term stability. The future, a growing, profitable future, that is, rests on Nissan's ability to produce innovative new products in America once again, reminiscent of the days in the 60s and 70s when the company changed the way people in the country viewed automobile manufacturing.

Ghosn acknowledges the stakes are high. Nissan is entering a volatile state to launch a new line of products, including full size pickup trucks, viewed as risky by more than a few for obvious reasons. But with a billion dollars now on the table in Mississippi, Ghosn isn't blinking, charging ahead in America with a mentality similar to that used by his Japanese predecessors at Nissan some fifty years before.

"The challenge is big," he said, "but we are coming from hell trying to get to purgatory. We have to make a difference and do it fast."

— oOo —

There is irony, of course, that Nissan's upward trek begins in a state still divided down the harshest line. It isn't lost on Ghosn, who learned quickly that traditions in the Magnolia State are closely held by masses on the inside slow to change. But Ghosn is hoping Mississippi, like Japan, is more adaptable than history and conventional wisdom suggest.

Appendix B

Author's Note: This is a proposal that my agent, Frank Weimann of The Literary Group, and I both agreed had a strong storyline worthy of a significant sale. But, although it generated some editor interest, I was never offered the type of money we felt it deserved and so the book remains unwritten and the story will likely never reach print. It is included here to show how good proposals represented by good agents often go unsold. The story was solid, the outline well-written and the marketing plan thorough, yet a deal could not be made—an example of difficulty in getting published, even for a seasoned author with a good proposal. The biggest problem with this proposal, editors told me, was the fact that most people are tired of reading about Henry Ford, considering he has been written about in literally hundreds of books. Still, it serves as an example of a non-fiction proposal for would-be authors to study.

——————————— oOo ———————————

oOo

Strange Bean
Henry Ford, His Scientist and the Birth of the World's Most Important Agricultural Crop
By David Magee

Overview

Henry Ford is best remembered as America's industrial pioneer for first envisioning mass production assembly and building cars affordable for the middle class in his manufacturing company. Embedded in history as the auto baron who "put the world on wheels," he is one of the most colorful, complicated and studied figures of the 20th century due to his life that was filled with fascinating accomplishment and paradox, engineering social change in a nation by doubling the wages of workers on a whim in one moment and battling them with an iron, confrontational fist the next.

His legend of industrial achievement and personal eccentricity has been well documented during the past 75 years, told in dozens of books which have sold hundreds of thousands of copies around the world. Historians, as well as the general public, understand the importance of the man and his automotive work because the car and large-scale manufacturing as we know it today is still rooted in many successes of his 1903 creation, the Ford Motor Company. Many also understand the complexity of the man, having been told through a recent best-selling book *Henry Ford and the Jews: The Mass Production of Hate* published by PublicAffairs in 2001) how his wild-eyed notions, like the one about the inferiority of Jews, led to obsessive preaching and propaganda-based expeditions.

oOo

———————————— oOo ————————————

The Henry Ford saga that remarkably has not been told, however, is one that dramatically changed the course of food consumption and production for the entire world beginning in the 1930s and helped launch a vitally-important movement known as "chemurgy," which uses chemistry and applied sciences to obtain more uses from agriculture. The book *Strange Bean: Henry Ford, His Scientist and the Birth of the World's Most Important Agricultural Crop* tells this story for the first time, resulting in a thoroughly-researched, highly-commercial read appealing to readers of contemporary history and those seeking to understand the important 20th century events that most affect our lives today.

With colorful detail obtained from hundreds of pages of research, cooperation from The Henry Ford museum which includes Ford's original Soybean Laboratory, and first-hand, never-before-granted interviews about the subject with members of the Ford family, *Strange Bean* tells how Henry Ford became obsessed with the under-utilized soy in the 1930s and almost single-handedly launched the legume into being the most world's most used, versatile and important agricultural crop.

The story begins with Henry Ford's quest as a young man to build a machine that made labor on the farm easier and more productive. Born on a Michigan farm in 1863, Ford was always troubled by the debilitating amount of labor required by families on the farm to barely scratch out a living. A self-taught engineer unable to read blueprints, Ford devoted years in an attempt to perfect farm equipment before finding intrigue near the turn-of-the century in the motorcar.

Once Ford Motor Company experienced unbridled success

———————————— oOo ————————————

—————————————————— oOo ——————————————————

after its founding in 1903 with the Model T, Ford's wealth and industrial pioneering never veered far from the farm as he wrestled with a sort of guilt that the explosion of American industry, fueled by his innovation and vision, was taking workers away from the farm and placing in jeopardy the fruitful future of agriculture. He had pride in the fact that his creation, the mass produced automobile, had proven to be the ultimate demise of the horse, but it also bothered him in the sense of how it might urbanize the rural landscape. When luring worker applicants to Ford Motor Company by the hundreds of thousands in 1914 with this announcement of the $5 wage, for instance, Henry Ford, once an oil-stained farmhand himself, reconciled with himself for taking employees away from lower-paying field jobs in droves by announcing publicly that Ford Motor Company would "henceforth arrange its production schedule so that layoffs would be made around harvest time" in hopes of inducing "our men to respond to the calls of the farmers for harvest hands." Even as his automobiles sold around the nation by the thousands he continued to develop and sell tractors in a quest to improve life on the farm.

As Ford Motor Company and other Detroit automakers grew larger and the metropolitan area began to grow and flourish with the economic advancement, Ford felt increasing angst about what appeared to be a pronounced movement in the country away from the strength of the farm. To foster a spirit of town and country discovery and unity, he began to build near the Ford Motor Company a network of "village industries" intended to bring harmony between town and country as workers and local farmers crafted together amid flowing streams, small

—————————————————— oOo ——————————————————

———————————— oOo ————————————

workshops and watermills. Such a set-up, he believed, would allow farmers to work at the rural industries during crop off-seasons.

With a personal wealth running into the billions and a well-established Ford Motor Company as a leading industrial force in America as the 1920s dawned, Henry Ford's inquisitive personality and desire to be an inventor led him on a constant quest to derive utility from the simplest items and create simplicity in the world's most difficult challenges. He was pleased to conceive of and actually build a manufacturing facility that could create entire, affordable automobiles in one single location from start to finish, shipping in iron ore on one end and spitting out finished product on the other the Rouge factory), but the process relied on limited, non-sustainable resources. What Ford yearned for was invention that *created* the resource used for input, resulting in harmony between industry, science and hopefully the farm. In 1921, after "nearly a year in silence," he predicted publicly that man-made products would replace the milk and meat from cows. Scientific meat, he said, was entirely possible. Scientific milk, he said, was entirely possible. If he could get rid of the horse as he had done with the automobile, certainly, he could get rid of the cow.

"It is a simple matter to take the same cereals that the cows eat and make them into a milk which is superior to the natural article and much cleaner," he said. "The cow is the crudest machine in the world."

Henry Ford's entrepreneurial and exploratory success had its advantages in regard to his voracious hunger to pursue new possibilities such as cow-less meat and milk. With a tight and

———————————— oOo ————————————

engaged circle of friends ranging from his closest, inventor Thomas Edison, to the Kellogg Brothers, to tire magnate Harvey Firestone and whoever the sitting President of the United States was at the time, Ford was able to share and receive ideas, knowledge and resources from the top inventors and leaders of early-20th century America. It was during a visit of Ford and Edison in the late 1920s to the health spa owned and run by Dr. John Harvey Kellogg in Battle Creek, Michigan that the auto baron was first acquainted with a plant called the soybean. One of the nation's leading food experts at the time, Kellogg had been introduced to the soybean during a fact-finding mission to Asia.

References to the soybean in China date back 5,000 years, suggesting the plant and its byproduct was among five or six of the most important crops. It was ancient Chinese farmers who coaxed the plant into upright growth and learned to soak soybeans in water to create a white, drinkable milk-like substance. So heavily used on a regular basis by Chinese citizens was soy milk that the beans which produced it were affectionately known as the "cow of China." But even though soybeans were for centuries a staple of the Asian diet, its uses were generally limited to the making of soymilk, tofu, soy flour used to make miso), and soy sauces. Few people outside of Asia cultivated the bean or cared for it.

It was not until 1804 that soybeans arrived in the U.S. when sailors brought a load from China to balance the weight of a ship. Upon arrival, the beans were dumped and the pile thinned as farmers throughout the country experimented growing the soy on a limited basis, using the beans to make soy sauce. More

———————————— oOo ————————————

frequently, however, the beans were merely grown for fertilizer purposes and then plowed under, back into the soil, since the plants possess the soil-enriching property of other leguminous plants with an ability to take nitrogen from the air and transfer it to the ground through its roots.

Limited research in the U.S. during the early 1900s found more uses for the soybean. In 1904, for instance, George Washington Carver who would become a friend and ally of Ford's) found that the soybean was useful in making oils and also had many protein benefits and its usage increased. Still, there were less than ten million bushels of soybeans in production in the United States and very few uses for the product in 1928 when Ford became obsessed with a new agricultural concept called "farm chemurgy," in which chemistry and allied sciences are partnered together to find uses for agriculture. Specifically, in what some detractors labeled as neurotic fantasy, Ford believed the products of the farm possessed many useful qualities for industry, they just merely needed discovering.

In the onset of the Great Depression in 1929, Henry Ford developed a laboratory in Dearborn, Michigan in the location of his "village industries"—which would become known as Greenfield Village—to conduct experiments in an effort to determine which agricultural products held the most promise for yielding industrial uses and additional, untapped food uses. Named the "Chemical Plant of the Edison Institute," the laboratory was manned by Ford's childhood friend Dr. Edsel Ruddiman for whom his only child was named). Also working on the plant was a young scientist named Robert Boyer. A graduate of the Henry Ford Trade School, Boyer met Ford while

———————————— oOo ————————————

ice skating one afternoon at the Dearborn Inn, run by his father and owned by Ford. As a student at Ford's "Place for Damn Fool Experiments," Boyer had learned and appreciated his quest to create new from the old and he excitedly went to work for Ford at the lab as the 1920s came to an end. Brought to Boyer, Ruddiman and others in the laboratory for study were harvests from the plants of Ford's surrounding cultivated experimental fields.

The nation's largest crop, corn, got the most attention at first, but it did not take long for Ford and his researchers to determine that while corn meal was highly valuable from continent to continent, the makeup of the kernel made corn a vegetable with limitation. Experiments continued, however, even as Ford Motor Company spiraled downward along with the rest of American industry as jobs evaporated in excruciatingly difficult conditions. To personally help facilitate and expedite the process, Henry Ford brought in used orange peels and bags of garbage from his home for study. He ordered the thousands of acres of land surrounding Ford Motor Company be planted in a variety of agricultural crops usable for experimentation.

Unemployment in Detroit approach 70 percent, but Ford pushed ahead with his chemurgistic ideals. If anything, the difficult industrial period pushed Ford into a deeper conviction that the farm held the key for many of the country's business ills. The country could not eat, purchase or use all that farmers could grow at the time and grain was being destroyed by the government simply to stabilize prices while many people could not even afford meat for the table.

The quest to find a myriad of uses for an agricultural plant

—————— ∘O∘ ——————

gained immeasurable momentum in the final weeks of 1931, however, when after emerging from deep mourning from the death of his dearest friend, Thomas Edison, earlier in the year and coming to terms that his company would survive the economic Depression, Henry Ford walked into the laboratory one night for one of his regular visits to ponder and pass time and found a copy of the book *The Soybean* 1923), written by C.V. Piper and W.J. Morse, employees of the United States Department of Agriculture who devoted their careers to promotion of the soybean despite its insignificance in the country at the time. The first English language work published on the soybean, the 323-page book contained a detailed history of the soybean dating to its Asian origin and including suggestions for Western recipes. The authors had never been to Asia, but through mail correspondence had obtained enough information to move Henry Ford to the point of utter conviction.

The day after reading the book in one sitting, Ford went into the greenhouse at the laboratory and told Boyer to get rid of everything, at once. "I'll be back in a few hours and I want everything out of here," he said. "From now on I don't want you to talk or think about working on anything but soybeans. That's the thing of the future."

Tests that had been underway for months on other agricultural items were swept up instantly in damaging fashion, shoveled hurriedly into boxes so the lab would be clear when the boss returned. Virtually unknown at the time, only ten million acres of soybeans were being grown in the United States and with the exception of some beans that were used to make soy sauce, most were simply plowed back into the ground for

—————— ∘O∘ ——————

their fertilization benefits. The plant, however, had gained in one night the full attention of the country's biggest industrialist who was moved by such endearing facts he had read, most notably that the soybean was rich in both oil and protein and the plant contained a useful, residual fiber. The fruit of the soy also stored well and was low in water content, desirable qualities for multiple uses. For Henry Ford, the epiphany translated to instantaneous adoration and obsession of this strange bean. He returned to the laboratory the next day after reading the book cover-to-cover with a truckload of soybean plants, dumping them outside the door.

Boyer, the one-time apprentice, was placed in charge of the Chemical Laboratory, which would soon be renamed the Soybean Laboratory, and running the assimilated group of scientists, which Ford referred to as "the boys." Though Boyer was but a young chemist with limited experience and none outside of the Edison Institute, Henry Ford trusted him without question, willing to fund any experiment or expedition as it related to the soybean. Ford's longtime friend, Dr. Edsel Ruddiman, continued work to work in the village, manning a nearby laboratory and continuing experiments with the soy, but other agricultural products as well. To support the fast-paced research, Ford ordered the 10,000 acres of land which comprised the Ford Farms in the surrounding Detroit planted in some 300 varieties of soybeans and he publicly urged farmers in Michigan to abandon other efforts to focus in the crop with the promise that it would "make them rich."

A soybean processing plant was built at Ford's Greenfield Village, which processed six tons of soybeans per day. The first

oOo

and certainly the most vindicating of work by the boys focused on were developing uses for Henry Ford's beloved soybean oil. After one year of experimentation and a $1.2 million investment, the laboratory had developed a very good paint that was based on soybean oil. Used on Ford cars a derivative is still by Ford today), the paint had an advantage over lacquer since when the soy-based paint dries, it does not leave small, hard-to-see pits which allows dirt and water to settle and cause premature peeling. The soybean paint proved to finish hard "like a plate" and provide a more durable surface. Boyer had also devised a first-ever solvent extraction procedure which allowed both soy protein and oil to be produced from the same beans, opening the door to prolific food and industrial use. Additionally, he and his co-workers had found a way to use leftover soybean meal in plastic, creating a horn that was suitable for use on Ford cars.

But work with the soybean was not limited to the industrial laboratory. Ford was talking about the plant to everyone everywhere he went, adamant that the bean would change the world. His personal chef, Jan Willemse, as well as Dr. Ruddiman, were given piles of newly-harvested beans each day and urged to create replicate popular menu choices of all types with items made from soy beans and plants. Ford was presented "tasty" dishes on a weekly, if not daily basis, and frequently urged Ford Motor Company executives to try them as well. He was so pleased with advances the boys had made in food items and oil production that he arranged for a major display at his "Industrialized American Barn" exhibit at the upcoming 1934 World's Fair in Chicago. "By now," wrote *Fortune* magazine in 1933, "Henry Ford) is as much interested in the Soya bean as he is in the

oOo

———————— oOo ————————

V-8." At the World's Fair, Ford made an international splash, wearing around a suit weaved from soy fibers and inviting if not forcing) journalists to sample is full-scale menu featuring food made from the soy.

Henry Ford's World's Fair Menu
Tomato juice seasoned with soy sauce
Celery stuffed with soybean cheese
Puree of soybean
Salted soybean
Soybean crackers
Soybean croquettes with tomato sauce
Buttered green soybeans
Pineapple ring with soybean cheese and soybean dressing
Soybean bread with soybean butter
Apple pie with soy crust
Cocoa with soymilk
Assorted soybean cookies, cakes, and candies
Roasted soybean coffee
Soymilk ice cream

The World's Fair guests were not particularly impressed, if at all, since many items were not palatable because of the tendency of soy oil to be slightly rancid. "Nothing we newsmen ate that day," a guest wrote years later, "led us to foresee that soybeans were destined to become an ingredient in many popular food products…" Still, the resulting publicity and creativity with the soy brought international attention. With an inventor and industrialist like Henry Ford so heavily focused on the promotion

———————— oOo ————————

of one underutilized agricultural item, the potential for wealth, many assumed, must exist. Following the successful World's Fair promotion, Henry Ford's commitment to the soybean and his passion for it grew exponentially.

His anxiety of proving his predictions of greatness for the product increased, however, and he began to push Bob Smith, one of "the boys," to find solutions for getting rid of the cow just as industry had gotten rid of the horse. Soymilk dated back to the earliest centuries in China, but its taste was not refined enough for American consumption on anything but the smallest scale. Ford urged Smith to devote one full laboratory specifically to the goal of "getting rid of the cow." In just a few months, a milk formula had been developed by dissolving the protein out of soybean meal instead of grinding it out, resulting in a much better tasting soymilk. Henry Ford tried it and was so pleased that he took out a little black notebook from his pocket and inscribed the words, "First good milk." Ford began to stop by for a drink of the milk every day, and even began asking for baked bread made from soy meal to go along with it.

With the advances made by Boyer in the Soybean Laboratory, Ford began to talk publicly of plans to expand the scope of the soybean beyond just food, however. Ford already had a soy protein fiber facility up and running and Boyer was developing methods that resulted in a thoroughly washed and tasteless product that promised to open doors for many protein-based food applications. To show the world the advances, Ford Motor Company set up a display at the 1938 World's Fair in New York that included a machine that could spin the soy protein fibers into this tasteless, moldable form.

———— oOo ————

Boyer had also made extensive progress implementing soy into plastics. Henry Ford was perhaps ahead of himself but genuinely hopeful when he began to talk publicly about company plans to build a plastic car. He was hailed in many circles. *The New York Times*, for instance, called the move something near genius, while others laughed and fond the soybean-based plastic car perfect joke fodder. *The Cleveland Press* wondered why Ford did not strengthen his plastic by adding spinach and *The St. Louis Glove Democrat* stated that the new vehicle, "part salad and part automobile," marked the triumph of the vegetable over the steel industry.

But by 1941, a year which saw the United States produce 78 million bushels of soybeans, Ford Motor Company did in fact produce a plastic car, although the importance of soy decreased in the plastic of the car body drastically from original plans because Boyer and fellow researchers could not make soy 100 percent waterproof. Soy, however, was a major element of other non-structural components of the car and it was highly-publicized around the world that the automobile was the result of Ford's work with the soybean. To celebrate, journalists were invited and served an all-soy luncheon. Afterward, a gangly, 77-year-old Henry Ford sought to demonstrate the strength of the plastic car by striking it on the trunk with an ax. To ease the blow, he used the blunt end and swung ever-so-slightly, but the point was made. The all-plastic, somewhat-soy car withstood the blow and Boyer drove it away as the crowd watched to emphasize the point.

Immediately after the display of the plastic car, much began to change for Henry Ford, the soybean and consumers. The

———— oOo ————

———————————— oOo ————————————

advent of World War II quickly killed the idea of a plastic car because they took too long to make and Ford's deteriorating health caused his distraction from the project. Also, armed with the top soybean development knowledge in the world, Ford's boys were beginning to move on to bigger and better things. Henry Ford, at the age of 80, sold his soybean operations to the Drackett Company in 1943. He would die just a few years later, to be imbedded in history as the man who put the world on wheels.

Bob Smith, Ford's scientist who perfected soymilk, opened a plant Delsoy Products) that used soymilk for a variety of whipped toppings and baked goods. One of his key workers, who had also previously worked at Ford, left for Rich Products in Buffalo, New York, where he led a commercial success of such products as coffee creams and whipped topping. Boyer went to work for the Drackett Company in 1943, which bought Ford's soy protein operations. Drackett sold its soybean operations to Archer Daniels Midland just six years later and Boyer went to another company, taking along his patent for man-made protein fibers based on the soybean. It took seven more years, but Boyer's patent was finally sold as a spinning license to Worthington Foods in 1956. By 1977, seven large food companies, including Worthington, General Mills and Nabisco, had licenses on the patent and products such as Bac*O's imitation bacon bits) and other popular imitation meat products reached the market. He and Ford shared dozens of soybean patents which were implemented by companies all over the world before expiring and falling to the general domain and even greater popularity.

By the 1970s, soybeans had become the second largest

———————————— oOo ————————————

volume crop in the United States, with more than one billion bushels being produced each year. Once little known and of little value, the soybean had turned to gold, with an American export value higher than anything else in the country, including jet aircraft, computers or the automobile. Today, the soybean is grown in more than two-thirds of the country and continues to be the most important crop in the world, with more than 100 uses in mainstream products, ranging from margarine and soymilk to cosmetics and plastics.

Research

The author is uniquely positioned to write this important historical story in a readable style due to his unequaled access to research archives. With cooperation from The Henry Ford museum and its curator in charge of agriculture and with interviews from Ford family members and Ford Motor Company historians, the author will recreate the scenery, the personality and the actions of Henry Ford and his scientist as they imagined and created ways the plant could provide a myriad of uses.

The author has access to more than 1,000 pages of research from articles published over more than 70 years that reveal the incredible story of how Henry Ford and his scientist gave birth to soybean as we know it today. The research originated during time the author spent in the Detroit area while researching for a year-and-a-half for his book *Ford Tough*.

During free time in the Detroit area, the author would go to The Henry Ford museum learning about the impact of Henry Ford and his fascination with the soybean. In conversations with members of the Ford family about their grandfather and great-grandfather, it became apparent that they considered the work he and his scientist conducted with the soybean to be among the most important of his life.

The author's research for *Strange Bean* includes:

- The Henry Ford Museum maintains archives of Henry Ford's Soybean Institute at Greenfield Village; curator of agriculture for the museum is cooperative.
- Ford Motor Company archives one of the world's most extensive corporate archives, the collection includes dozens of items relating to Henry Ford, his scientist and their soybean research.
- More than 500 articles containing information about Henry Ford, scientist Robert Boyer and their work in regard to the soybean. Included are extensive interviews with Ford, Boyer and others who worked with the industrialist and scientist.
- Dozens of transcripts from interviews with Boyer, Smith and other key scientists who were key parts of Henry Ford's soybean movement.
- Interviews with the family of Robert Boyer, who was Henry Ford's scientist and ultimately the foremost authority on the soybean and its potential uses.
- Interviews with international soy foods researches and experts William Shurtleff and Akiko Aoyagi.
- John Deere archives author wrote *The John Deere Way*, to be published in March 2005 by Wiley, and has spent time in company archives with substantial information regarding emergence of the soybean and its importance as a global agricultural crop.

Approach/Delivery

Using crisp style with careful attention to full character development and framing of the times, *Strange Bean* will be a 100,000-word manuscript that accurately and colorfully portrays one of the more historic movements in the 20th century United States.

Since the majority of research has already been conducted and all that remains are first-hand interviews, the manuscript will be delivered exactly six months from contract.

The Author

David Magee is a non-fiction author with a passion for telling untold stories that shape or have shaped our lives with flair. A member of the American Society of Journalists and Authors, Magee's book, *Turnaround: How Carlos Ghosn Rescued Nissan* (HarperCollins; January 2003) has sold almost 100,000 copies in eight languages.

He is also the author of *Ford Tough: Bill Ford and the Battle to Rebuild America's Automaker* (Wiley; 2004), which is currently being translated into three languages (Korean, Simple Chinese, and Russian); *The John Deere Way: Performance That Endures* (Wiley; February, 2005); and *Endurance: Winning Life's Majors The Phil Mickelson Way* (Wiley; March, 2005).

A former newspaper editor and columnist, business owner, city councilman and advertising executive, Magee is the founder of Jefferson Press (www.jeffersonpress.com), a small publisher that has worked with and published such authors as Larry Brown, Barry Hannah, Tom Franklin and Will Campbell.

Formerly of Oxford, Mississippi, David Magee's (www .david-magee.com) love of writing and books developed from relationships in the South's most literary small town, including Dean Faulkner Wells, Larry Well, Larry Brown, John Grisham and former American Booksellers Association President Richard Howorth. He currently lives with his wife and three children on Lookout Mountain, Tennessee.

Marketing

No book has ever been written about Henry Ford, his scientist and their strange-but-successful experiments and promotion with the world's most important agricultural crop, the soybean. *Strange Bean* tells this historic story in a fast-paced, character-driven style similar to mass appeal, best-selling history books like *Isaac's Storm: A Man, A Time, and the Deadliest Hurricane Ever* (Crown; 1999) and *Devil in the White City: Murder, Magic, and Madness at the Fair That Changed America* (Crown; 2003) by Erik Larson. Other examples include *The Professor and the Madman: A Tale of Murder, Mystery, and the Making of the Oxford Dictionary* (HarperCollins; 1998) and *The Map That Changed the World: William Smith and the Birth of Modern Geology* (HarperCollins; 2001) by Simon Winchester.

With Borders stores headquarters located in Ann Arbor, Michigan, the book has natural appeal to the sales force of one of the county's larger bookselling chains because of its Detroit-area roots and the author has recognition in this region as well. And internationally, the soybean is used and consumed all over the world creating curiosity for this strange but useful bean. This, combined with Henry Ford's studied and recognized historical name make this story one with global appeal.

Brazil, for example, has experienced its rapid economic growth

———————————————————— oOo ————————————————————

in recent years largely on the strength of soybean production and this emerging market is an excellent example of bookselling opportunities abroad. The soybean is also originally from Asia and is still the top and most important crop, giving the story appeal in Japan, China and other countries in the Far East.

Closer to home, the soybean and its byproducts are a significant part of the daily lives of so many and most of its uses relate directly to the work and vision of pioneers Henry Ford and his scientist, Robert Boyer, making the book a natural acquisition by all public and academic libraries, a key installment in American history and a smooth yet informative read for book buyers everywhere.

———————————————————— oOo ————————————————————

Acknowledgements

More than anyone else, my wife is primarily responsible for my decision and commitment to be a full-time author. For her belief that I could do it and for her never-ending support despite some times that were exceedingly difficult, I am most grateful.

I am also appreciative of Jefferson Press editor Henry Oehmig, who took the time to read this manuscript and make suggestions. Our aim from the beginning was to write and produce a book that gives simple answers to a very complex and difficult subject. On some level, I think we achieved that.

Others who have played a role in the development and publication of this book who deserve mention are Charlotte Lindeman, a Jefferson Press partner and the director of sales and marketing, and book cover and interior designer Fiona Raven (www.fionaraven.com). Ms. Raven has become a trusted and valuable source for Jefferson Press and I am thankful for her many contributions.

Finally, I want to thank my friends at Independent Publishers Group (www.ipgbook.com) in Chicago for supporting Jefferson Press with the full extent of their abilities and for serving as a trustworthy and reliable business partner. Specifically, Mary Rowles has been a constant source of feedback and support and I am grateful.

oOo